THE EXETER-SQUAMSCOTT

River of Many Uses

Bog Bridge, Fremont. c. 1910. Matthew E. Thomas Collection.

Copyhold Mills, Brentwood-Fremont line, c. 1863. Matthew E. Thomas Collection.

THE EXETER-SQUAMSCOTT
River of Many Uses

BY OLIVE TARDIFF

Published for

The Rockingham Land Trust and Exeter River Local Advisory Committee

by
Peter E. Randall Publisher
Portsmouth, New Hampshire
2004

Additional copies available from:
Exeter River Local Advisory Committee (ERLAC)
C/O Rockingham Planning Commission
156 Water Street
Exeter, NH 03833
603-778-0885

Peter E. Randall Publisher
Box 4726, Portsmouth, NH 03802
www.perpublisher.com

Cover credit: painting courtesy of Michael Seekamp. A biologist
who minored in art, he lives in Newton, New Hampshire, and is a
principal with his brother at Seekamp Environmental Consulting
in Kingston, New Hampshire.

Introduction

to the New Edition

There is clearly an argument to be made that the Exeter and Squamscott Rivers are in actuality a single river. In the late afternoon hours in the usually studious research room of the Exeter Historical Society, the volunteer staff, tired of the unending transcription work sent to them by an unyielding curator, will begin again the debate—one river or two? From a mapmaker's point of view, it appears as one clearly defined river snaking its way ever eastward from Chester until it twists to the north and flows into Great Bay. If one didn't observe the water closely, it would seem to be a single stream.

But maps do not show the *direction* or *composition* of the waters so carefully colored blue. If they did, it would be impossible to avoid the differences between the tidal brackish Squamscott and the steady freshwater Exeter. The water in the Exeter River rolls into town, bringing with it all the bits and pieces of places to the west. Tiny twigs, small fish, silt, melted snow, all find their way to the falls in the center of Exeter. A myriad of tales from the woodland creatures, unspoken, travel to the sea and the wider world. The Exeter River possesses, in its movement, potential power that the early Europeans viewed eagerly. This river could be put to use.

Generations of native people, however, had already been using the river, but not because of its movement. As the Exeter River tumbles down the falls, it leaves behind the woodlands and meets the world at large. The water at the base of the falls comes in and out of town with the tide. Pulled by the moon twice a day, the Squamscott River shifts direction as the water moves to the north, to the south. It brings with it animals and plant life that comfortably straddle the worlds and ecosystems of salt and fresh water. The tribes who gave the river its name used the Squamscott as a seasonal source for food. Europeans would use it as a highway to the Atlantic shipping routes.

The account book of Exeter merchant, John Giddings, tells a tale of the two rivers. He sold imported goods over a period of years from 1765 until 1781. Townspeople ran up accounts for sugar, rum, molasses, limes, and English cloth and paid for it with lumber, fish, and barrel staves. The Exeter powered the mills that produced the goods. The Squamscott supplied the egress to the outside world.

Over the centuries, the Exeter and Squamscott Rivers have been fished, weired, dredged, dammed, straightened, fouled, and cleaned. As new technologies have lessened the economic power of the falls, the rivers have returned to their natural states. The wildlife has returned and as one walks along the continuous riverbanks, the change at the falls becomes more obvious. Seagulls give way to ducks.

And we return to our late afternoon debate—one river or two? I imagine I've always thought of the two rivers as being very individual. The Exeter River seems local—my own neighborhood. The fresh water is sweet, like rainfall. The Squamscott has higher aspirations. It is the wilder international traveler, its waters undrinkable yet life sustaining on a more cellular level. They meet at a drop in the landscape currently occupied by a local library—another place where one's quiet internal world can be broadened to wider horizons. The falls are the best place to contemplate the debate.

Barbara Rimkunas, Curator,
Exeter Historical Society
Exeter, 2004

Rockingham Land Trust
8 Center Street, Exeter, NH 03833

The Rockingham Land Trust was established in 1980 as a membership-based, non-profit organization dedicated to conserving the farms, forestland, and water resources of greater Rockingham County. The Trust works with landowners, local governments, and other natural resource protection organizations to identify and preserve the region's natural resources and scenic landscape. The fields, forests, and rivers of our region are a treasure as well as a responsibility for the people who live here or visit.

Exeter River Local Advisory Committee
C/O Rockingham Planning Commission
156 Water Street, Exeter, NH 03833

The Exeter River Local Advisory Committee (ERLAC) was established in 1996 to develop and oversee a management plan for the Exeter River corridor. ERLAC includes representatives from the ten Exeter River watershed communities: Chester, Sandown, Danville, Fremont, Raymond, Brentwood, Exeter, East Kingston, Kingston, and Kensington. The "Exeter River Corridor and Watershed Management Plan" was developed by ERLAC with the advice and participation of community representatives, federal, state and local government agencies, and private citizens. The plan is about people working together to understand what it takes to improve, maintain, and enhance the quality of their watershed, and about charting a course that will ensure a healthy and viable river and watershed well into the future.

Greater Piscataqua Community Foundation
446 Market Street, Portsmouth, NH 03801

The Greater Piscataqua Community Foundation is the oldest and largest regional division of the New Hampshire Charitable Foundation. It has grown from serving nine communities in 1983 to forty-one communities today. In the last twenty years, the Greater Piscataqua Foundation has awarded more than $17.5 million in grants and scholarships to support a wide range of community needs. The GPCF matches the interests of its donors with community needs in order to improve the quality of life in its service area.

Dale Brothers Mill, Chester. Melissa Rosetti Collection.

Edwards Mill and Lumber Yard, Chester. Melissa Rosetti Collection.

Black Rocks Mills, Fremont c. 1905. Matthew E. Thomas Collection.

Crawley Falls Dam, Brentwood, Morrill House in the background, c. 1907.
Matthew E. Thomas Collection.

Up-and-Down sawmill, Sandown, 1903. Matthew E. Thomas Collection.

CONTENTS

Cavil Mills–John M. Brown's mill, c. 1870–75, Fremont. Mill at right also shown on page 63. Matthew E. Thomas Collection.

Acknowledgments

D ozens of people have helped in this project. Several have read all or part of the manuscript and suggested important changes.

Dr. Donald H. Chapman spent considerable time explaining the geology of the river. Eugene Finch, Donald Foster, and William White were most generous with information about Indian life. Matthew (Sandy) Thomas shared his research materials on mills and guided me on a tour of millsites in Fremont, Brentwood, and Sandown.

Nancy Merrill's notes taken from *Exeter News-Letters* and her knowledge of local history were invaluable. The chapter on shipbuilding owes much to William Saltonstall's diligent research and extensive writings.

Without the steady support and thoughtful judgment of my husband, Joseph Tardiff, this book could not have been written.

Thank you all.

Olive Tardiff

1979

INTRODUCTION

The river was here long before the people came. Before the river there was ice.

We will never know whether the river known to us by two names – the Exeter and the Squamscott – flows in a channel that existed many millions of years ago when New England first began to take shape, or whether the forces of the Great Ice Age radically altered its course.

Scientists tell us that New Hampshire already had a permanent land area when the first ice sheets descended from the north 2,000,000 years ago, although our granite hills had been alternately thrust up through the earth's crust, then worn down by erosion. Valleys had widened, then narrowed, with the flow of run-off water from mountain tops that carried soil and rocks to lower elevations.

We do know that the fourth and most recent glacier covered our area, and indeed all of New England, with a sheet of ice about 10,000 feet thick, concealing even the top of Mount Washington. The enormous weight of that glacier turned the ice beneath into a sluggish mass that slowly advanced southeastward to the sea, carrying with it sand, clay and silt as well as rocks of various sizes to be redistributed along its course.

The moving ice left its indelible imprints on New Hampshire's landscape. It scooped out hollows for lakes and carved its way through bedrock to create falls and rapids. Its huge mass caused the land beneath to sag. It deposited the gravel that is found so extensively in Exeter, Brentwood, Fremont, Raymond, Danville, and Sandown, the towns through which the river flows after rising in Chester.

About 13,000 years ago, the climate began to change. It warmed to about the temperatures of today, with considerable rainfall to speed along the process of melting New Hampshire's cover of ice. As the melt waters ran off into the ocean, land along the coast released from the weight of the glacier began to rise, while at the same time the sea level was elevated enough by melt water to spread inland as far as present-day Route 125. The incoming flow of salt water brought with it a marine blue clay that was deposited along the banks of tidal estuaries.

"Gradually," said Dr. Donald Chapman, retired University of New Hampshire geologist, "the rate of the rise of the land exceeded the rate of return of water from melting ice." The coast of New Hampshire began to take its present form.

As in other towns in the Piscataqua basin, the flow of water from the sea was eventually halted at the falls created by glacial action that had heaped up boulders and dug channels for fresh water flowing from the mountains. The Squamscott, as the river below these falls has come to be known, was described by Exeter historian Charles Bell as one of the five fingers of the Piscataqua that include the Lamprey, Oyster, Bellamy, and Newichewannock Rivers, with Great Bay forming the palm of the hand, while the wrist is the Piscataqua proper.

The present use of the name Squamscott, with the Exeter River, which rises at an elevation of 430 feet above sea level in a group of spring-fed ponds, has had several names. To those who live along the upper river, it has traditionally been known as the Exeter (although in Sandown it was once known as Merrymeeting River). To those who live in Exeter, it has sometimes been called the Fresh (as opposed to the Salt) River, or the Great to distinguish it from the Little River that feeds into it above the falls. At one time the entire length of approximately 45 miles was registered on maps as the Exeter River.

The present use of the name Squamscott, with varied spellings, for the lower river clarifies the division between the fresh water and the salt, with the line drawn at what has been called Great Falls in the heart of Exeter. The river's earliest inhabitants, the Indians, referred to the entire stream as Msquam-s-kook, often translated as "at the salmon place" or "big water place." More recently, J. Parkman Coffin of the N.H. Archeological Society has offered the interpretation, "river of the tidal marshes."

The fresh river twists and turns its way for about 34 miles from Chester to the Great Falls in Exeter. Its slightly brownish waters (tinted by leaves and bark from overhanging trees) flow smoothly and silently over beds of sand and gravel, ripple over glacial debris of shale and granite, and fall with force over ledges gouged out of bedrock. Whenever the drop in height is great enough, sufficient waterpower was available for the needs of colonists who settled near the river, and for the number of mills that were established in the 18th and 19th centuries.

As the post-glacial period climate became stabilized and temperatures rose to about present day levels, plants and animals once again moved northward. Forests grew tall where ice had once stunted and destroyed them. Game, large and small, roamed the area, and edible plants flourished. Shad, salmon, and alewives resumed their long treks from the sea to struggle over falls from salt to fresh water to lay their eggs. Eels in the lower river, and bass, trout, and pickerel in the upper were an ample food supply.

It was time, about 11,000 years ago, for human beings to appear on the river scene.

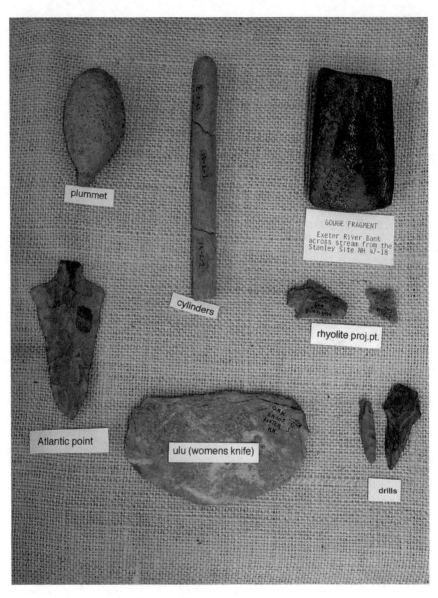

plummet

cylinders

GOUGE FRAGMENT

Exeter River Bank
across stream from the
Stanley Site NH 47-18

rhyolite proj.pt.

Atlantic point

ulu (womens knife)

drills

Stanley Site Artifacts. Courtesy of PEA.

❧

FIRST INHABITANTS ON THE ON RIVER

The first people to live along the river we now call the Exeter-Squamscott must have appreciated its bounty. The narrow stream that rose in a small pond only a few miles from the broad Merrimack region of New Hampshire, and to the river they named Msquam-s-kook, widened considerably as it neared the distant sea. The gentle flow of the upper river was interrupted by tumbling falls to be leaped by silver-sided salmon and other anadromous fish struggling upstream from the ocean to fresh-water spawning grounds.

Bears roamed the area, and there were large herds of deer. Squirrels chattered, turkeys squawked, and flocks of migrating pigeons darkened the sky for hours. Fish in both salt and fresh water appeared to be in almost limitless supply. The deep forest that crowded the river banks would provide for generations all the firewood needed for warmth and cooking.

The people we know as Squamscott Indians are believed to have descended from the aborigines who had crossed the Bering Land Bridge at least 30,000 years ago. Continuing slowly across the continent, they reached at last the shores of the Atlantic. Their long journey had brought some of them to the coastal region of New Hampshire, and to the river they called Msquam-s-kook.

Exactly how long ago these first visitors came, or by what route they entered the river basin, will perhaps never be known. Our environment is too hostile for preservation of significant artifacts which would provide clues. New Hampshire's acid soil and its climate caused a rapid deterioration of soft materials such as deerhide and woven reeds. Fragments of pottery, and stone or bone implements are about all that could withstand thousands of years of burial in the ground.

Only in this century have truly scientific methods been used to locate and date Indian sites in the Exeter area. In the past, random finds often went unidentified, and no attempt was made to record the exact spot or depth where they were discovered. Farmers often turned up arrowheads and other projectile points as they plowed their ground. Children picked up artifact with no understanding of their worth as historical evidence of an Indian past.

To a handful of Exeter people we owe the few systematic collections that have been preserved. Notable among them was the late Laurence Crosbie, teacher of English at Phillips Exeter Academy (PEA), who recognized the value of his finds and developed a collection of artifacts. Most of these Crosbie willed to PEA, intending them to be placed in a museum in Phillips Hall.

Crosbie encouraged the individual efforts of William White, an Exeter native, who since boyhood had taken an interest in exploring for Indian tools and weapons, mostly found on the surface of plowed farmland. Over the years, White has assembled a large collection of projectile points, pottery shards, plummets, and net sinkers, as well as tools that may have been used to shape bone, horn, and stone implements.

Others who contributed to the knowledge of the way Indians lived along the Exeter-Squamscott River have been Howard Sargent, who did considerable digging at Pickpocket Falls, and Solon Colby, known as "Mr. Indian of New Hampshire" because of his life-long search for Indian artifacts in this state. Eugene Finch, former English instructor, and Donald Foster, current anthropology instructor, both of PEA, have also used scientific methods to study and excavate sites in this area. Foster, with the aid of his students, and often using information supplied by Finch and White, has explored the oldest known Exeter River Indian encampments.

Indians had probably been in contact with Europeans in the northeast even before the travels of Giovanni Verazzano in the 16th century, and those of Captain John Smith, Martin Pring, and Samuel de Champlain in the 17th century. It is believed that as early as A.D. 900 the Vikings had found their way to the fertile fishing grounds of Nova Scotia, and had perhaps ventured as far south as Cape Cod.

While the Norsemen, as well as Breton and Portuguese fishermen, left no evidence of actual settlement, they may have stayed long enough to introduce lighter skins and hair color to the normally dark native population. They also left a legacy of trade, creating an early interest among the Indians in exchanging furs for manufactured goods. It was a practice that would be capitalized on by French traders of the 17th century, when they came here seeking fish and furs.

The theory that Indians came to New Hampshire about 11,000 years ago is now generally accepted, and the year 7000 B.C. seems the most likely for the Exeter-Squamscott River sites. Finch's, Foster's, and White's findings at the Stanley site off Linden Street and those of Finch and White in other locations have been of the Late Archaic and Woodland Eras, from about 1500 B.C. to A.D. 1600.

Although Foster has found little evidence that Woodland Indians were sedentary villagers, Pring reported in 1603 that he could see Indians at work on gardens along New England shores. Foster believes that those who stayed in the vicinity of Exeter were semi-nomadic hunters, gatherers, and fishermen. His conclusions are borne out by the many lithic materials brought in from other known sites.

It is impossible to reconstruct fully the culture of our Squamscott Indians, perhaps a sub-tribe of the southern New Hampshire Penacooks, who used the Algonquian language. The recorded observations of Europeans in the 1600s, and evidence from other sites in a better state of preservation, indicate certain skills and customs that we may assume were practiced by those who camped near the Msquam-s-kook.

In the Woodland period, Indians apparently traveled easily from one area to another. By moving frequently, they did not over-use a single species of plant or animal life. Since they lived by the seasons, it is logical to expect that they took advantage of each season's offerings.

The spruce or elm bark panels, cut and fitted by the women, could easily be removed from the basic pole framework of a conical wigwam, rolled up, and carried. While Indian males, in preparation for travel to the next campsite, packed their stone tools and weapons into birch bark canoes or the more utilitarian dugouts hollowed out of oak, pine, or chestnut tree trunks, women with their babies strapped to their backs took to the trails on foot, carrying household goods.

Many trails that would later become the winding roads of New Hampshire criss-crossed through the woods and followed rivers. Chester B. Price, in *Historic Indian Trails of New Hampshire*, described the

Pentucket Trail, no doubt often used by the Squamscotts, which ran from Pentucket or "Place of the Arrows" (now Haverhill, Massachusetts) to Kingston, and from there to Pickpocket Falls, then on to Exeter's Great Falls. Another trail followed the Exeter River through Brentwood.

Archeological evidence shows that the Squamscotts must have looked for sites that offered protection, access to the river, and an abundance of food. Artifacts found at the sites indicate that they camped, at least during the spring rush of fish from the sea, at Great Falls. They usually chose rather high ground, as at the Newfields site.

If an area had been cleared for the planting of vegetables by natural forces such as storms or infestations of insects, it might be selected for a summer settlement. River transportation and a good stand of trees were equally important.

A special feature of the Stanley site, according to Foster, was the presence of rhyolite and quartz rock which could be worked into projectile points as well as other functional articles. So many flakes and chips have been found there that Foster has concluded that this was a special activities site or maintenance factory.

Finch and White's discovery in 1959 of stone hoes and mortars in Newfields and at other locations would indicate that the Squamscotts did indeed practice farming. The corn and beans they planted would ripen before the first frost, and squash could survive freezing temperatures. All of the vegetables were an important supplement to the Indian diet that consisted mainly of plants, berries, nuts, fish, and game.

In 1955, White, while working near Pickpocket Falls, discovered pottery and stone fragments. Excavations at the site by members of the N.H. Archeological Society turned up three styles of pottery. Stone-lined hearths, tools, and projectile points were also found.

The presence of large game, used for food, clothing, shelter, and implements of bone and horn, was essential to the Woodland Indians. It is possible that caribou were still plentiful in the area and most certainly deer and bear abounded.

Hunting in those primeval forests required great skill and endurance, since the only weapons other than bows and arrows were crude javelins and spears to which pointed stones were attached. These had to be thrown with enough force to pierce an animal's hide. Sometimes hunters dug pits and covered them with leaves to trap unwary beasts. An easier method was to create snares with overhead branches fastened in such a way that the animal would be lifted and choked by a noose of plaited thongs.

Attacking large animals at close range with hand-thrown weapons was extremely hazardous. Hunters had to be very strong and swift; their aim had to be absolutely accurate. Heavy underbrush would impede their escape if a wounded animal turned on them or if an angry mate lurked nearby. Hunting sometimes demanded days of tracking, running almost constantly, with only a minimal food supply.

European observers apparently felt the Indian women were exploited and did most of the work while the men lazed about the camp. But Indian males would have needed to prepare weapons for the chase, construct canoes or dugouts, and strengthen their bodies for the ordeals of the hunt or battles with hostile tribes.

Ocean fishing, carried on mostly by the men, was also a dangerous pursuit. Leaning from easily tipped boats, they had to sink their crude harpoons into swiftly moving seals, porpoises, or whales. Sometimes they searched out sturgeons at night. Fortunately Indians were strong swimmers. Roger Williams wrote in 1643 that he had seen men swimming a mile from shore.

Smaller game and birds were easier prey. Women and children could hunt down the numerous squirrels, chipmunks, and rabbits that would furnish a quick meal. The millions of migrating pigeons that even in Colonial times were said to have darkened the skies for hours in their flight were trapped with nets fashioned from vines. Game birds were so plentiful they could be knocked down with sticks from their perches in trees.

Women's duties kept them close to the campsite. With the help of children, they picked berries of all kinds in season. In the fall, they gathered nuts from beech, hazel, hickory, butternut, and chestnut trees. The work of squaws was never done. When not preparing meals over the campfire, they were getting food ready for cooking.

Corn had to be pounded into meal, a most time-consuming task. A rock with a natural hollow in it could sometimes be found to use as a mortar with a stone pestle, but more often it was necessary to gouge out a stone or tree stump. Stews and soups were boiled by dropping stones heated in the fire into a birchbark pot. Meat and fish could be baked in ashes, broiled on sticks over an open fire, or simply eaten raw.

A common method of collecting fish would have been by trapping them in weirs made by weaving vines through stakes sunk deep into the

THE EXETER-SQUAMSCOTT RIVER

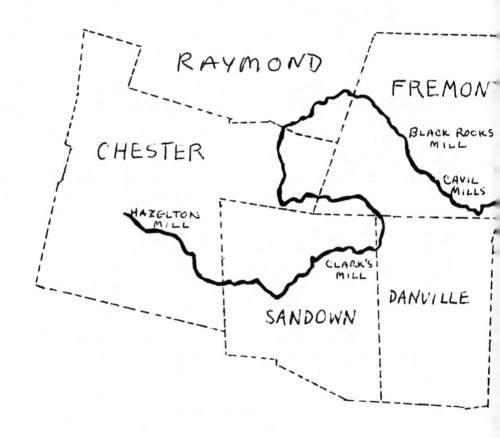

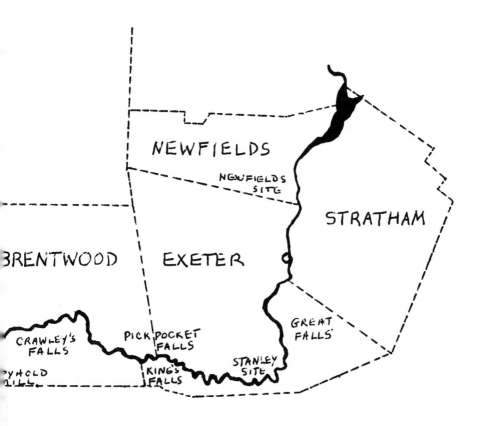

NEWFIELDS

NEWFIELDS
SITE

STRATHAM

BRENTWOOD

EXETER

CRAWLEY'S
FALLS

PICK POCKET
FALLS

GREAT
FALLS

STANLEY
SITE

KING'S
FALLS

PYHOLD
ILL

EXETER-SQUAMSCOTT
RIVER

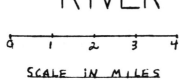

0   1   2   3   4

SCALE IN MILES

Map drawn by J. Tardiff

mud of the salt river. During the spring and fall migrations, women might have helped to net salmon and to gather the eels that clung to the muddy bottom of the river. Eels were so plentiful that it was possible to "tread" them out of brooks and pick them up by hand. Clams and oysters were dug out of the Squamscott at low tide.

To reach the ocean where multitudes of fish were borne in on spring tides, Indian men may have put their canoes or dugouts into the Taylor River near the present Route 88, paddling down to Hampton Harbor; or perhaps they made the long journey across Great Bay and down the treacherous Piscataqua. Women would have accompanied the men to the shore, in order to help salt and dry each day's catch.

Once the seafood had been safely preserved, women could turn their attention to the important work of collecting herbs for medicines and grasses for basket-making, and of planting vegetables. Where no cleared ground was available, the planters would drop three or four kernels of corn or a handful of dried beans into spaces between trees.

To kill a tree so that it could be more easily removed for planting space, it was common to pile wood around the trunk and burn it. In a slower process, trees were girdled by cutting notches all the way around. In about three years the dead tree could be cut down more easily with crude stone hatchets. Each year fields were burned over to increase the fertility of the soil. Sometimes those fires got out of control, doing widespread damage.

As soon as children were old enough to help, they would have been taught which herbs to gather for drying. Among their tasks would have been the carrying of water for cooking, and snaring small game. Roots of plants were a popular addition to the stewpot, and the various berries gave flavor and food value to ground cornmeal.

When large animals were killed near the campground, women would have been expected to help cut up the carcasses and carry the edible pieces back to the cooking area. It was their task, too, to cure the hide and soften it for use in making cold-weather clothing, bedding, and insulation for the interior of the wigwam. Bone and horn implements indicate that women stitched together the garments worn in cold weather. During the summer months, both men and women apparently wore only girdles around their waists, while children went completely naked.

When the days grew shorter and the harvest celebrations were over, the Squamscotts would begin to get ready for departure to winter quarters. They would carry as much food as possible, and bury the remainder for future use. The summer's accumulation of foods, skins, and tools was loaded onto their watercraft and onto the backs of women and older children. Then they would head for inland rivers and the higher elevations. There they could be assured of deep snows that would offer some protection against cold winds and provide easier tracking of large animals. These would be pursued by hunters on snowshoes until the exhausted prey dropped in the snow, to be finished off quickly.

By adapting both lifestyle and food habits to their environment, the Late Woodland Indians maintained a state of health that to Europeans seemed extraordinary. It was observed that Indians had clear, smooth skins, fine teeth, and well-muscled bodies, and showed no signs of disease or deformity. However, between 1615 and 1619, disaster struck New England Indians in the form of some as yet undetermined virulent disease. Thousands of lives were lost in an epidemic that swept the region. The total population was reduced from an estimated 70,000 to only about 18,000 by 1630.

It is believed that they were infected by early visitors to New England shores who brought ailments to which the Indians had developed no immunity. Many of those who survived illness fled to the comparative safety of St. Francis Indian encampments in Canada. Others died in the raids of enemy Mohawks who made regular forays into New England.

In any case, it was a pitifully small group, perhaps numbering no more than two or three thousand, that met the first settlers in New England. "God," declared John Winthrop of the Massachusetts Bay Colony, "hath hereby cleared our title to this place."

It made the acquisition of land by John Wheelwright and his followers relatively simple. In asking for the signatures of Wehanownowit and his men, they were dealing with a small number of natives who, if necessary, could have been easily overpowered. Moreover, the Squamscotts had no concept of land ownership.

"The Indian people never placed any interest in individual ownership of land," said a 1977 publication of the Pennacook Inter-tribal Nation called *Historic Indian-Colonial Relations of New Hampshire*. "Their belief that the Earth is their Mother, the source of Creation…would have prevented them from selling their ancestral lands." They expected just to share with the colonists, but, the publication pointed out, "the result was that the white man put up fences, dissected the land, and killed the wildlife of the forest and the fish in the streams."

Lillian Bailey, in her book *Up and Down New Hampshire*, has written that there was no need for aggression on the part of the colonists; the Indians could have been destroyed simply by removing their source of game.

Within just a few years, our Exeter settlers had the land virtually to themselves. Chief Wehananowit took his people westward, away from the banks of their Msquam-s-kook River, abandoning forever their traditional home.

CHAPTER II

6උ

PUTTING THE RIVER TO WORK

The little band of men who sailed up the Squamscott to sign a deed with Wehanownowit, his son Primadockyon, and others in the spring of 1638 must have been a hardy lot, physically strong, and equally strong in their convictions. There was grueling work ahead in making a settlement, and they needed to believe that they could establish in this wilderness a community of people who would live in peace and prosperity with their Indian neighbors.

Their leader, the Reverend John Wheelwright, a political and religious exile from Massachusetts Bay Colony, was a man to be trusted with this mission. He was a graduate of Cambridge University, and was once described by schoolmate Oliver Cromwell as a "formidable opponent" in football. Like his sister-in-law, Anne Hutchinson, Wheelwright was determined to put his own brand of Puritanism into practice.

Wheelwright is believed to have spent the winter of 1637-38 either at Strawbery Banke or with Edward Hilton, who had built a log cabin on the Squamscott about four miles below the falls. No doubt Wheelwright took the opportunity to study the terrain and choose the most desirable site for his settlement of Exeter.

In the spring of 1638, twenty men accompanied Wheelwright upriver to Great Falls—seven for religious reasons, the other thirteen, recent immigrants from England, ready to lend their skills to open up a new frontier.

According to a persistent legend, three men, Ralph Hall, Thomas Leavitt, and Thomas Wilson, already settled in the area for some time, were on hand to greet the newcomers. Their experience in collecting and preserving fish and trapping beaver for pelts to be traded abroad would have been invaluable to Wheelwright and his followers.

Until fields could be cleared and crops planted, fish was the most important staple in the colonists' diet. Moreover, it provided a base for trading in the grains, tools, and other goods needed for their own use and for dealing with the Indians.

The early settlers must have lived at first in wigwams until they could build the log cabins needed to house their families. Within a few months, women, children, and domestic animals arrived, transported by "coasters" (small sailing vessels with a crew of two or more men) from the Massachusetts Bay Colony. In 1639, uplands, marshes, and meadows were divided among these family units, which soon increased in number as even more colonists came to the settlement.

Wheelwright had chosen his acreage well. Under terms of the April 3, 1638 deed signed with the Squamscotts, Wheelwright and his followers could claim land from the Merrimack River in Massachusetts north to Oyster River, and running west to include the present towns of Epping, Fremont, and Brentwood. In return, the Indians received an unspecified sum of money and goods, and retained their rights to traditional hunting and fishing grounds.

All too soon, the deep forest to which the Indians retreated each fall were to be exploited for masts and lumber. The fresh river that slid over ledges on its way to the tidal basin would be dammed up, hampering the spring migrations of salmon, its waters converted to powder for grist, oil, and lumber mills. Log buildings would crowd the banks of the river; fields of lush grass, shoulder-high, would be plowed and planted with crops for the exclusive use of the colonists.

The role of the Great River was no longer to be that of supporting a primitive society, but of providing for the needs of a growing, industrialized community. As Timothy Dwight wrote in 1796, "A people who loved property little were overwhelmed by a people who loved it much."

Wheelwright, a professed man of God, probably never intended to deprive his red brothers of their livelihood. Perhaps he never fully understood the difference between his view of property and that of the Indians. Few Europeans did. It must have appeared as if all could share in nature's limitless bounty.

In an *Exeter News-Letter* article of May 13, 1927, Louis G. Hoyt, a local historian, wrote that two things were necessary to attract settlers to a community. One was a centrally located church, and the other was "the creation and development of a waterpower on a river where there was a natural fall that could be dammed to form a pond so that a sufficient head could be established to drive a waterwheel."

Exeter was fortunate in having both, and in being led by a man like Wheelwright who gave not only spiritual guidance, but practical leadership as well. With the Combination of 1639, an agreement signed by the settlers, he helped create an independent commonwealth and guaranteed a stable government.

It was Great Falls, of course, that had drawn Wheelwright and his followers to the banks of the Squamscott. The uses of waterpower had been known for thousands of years; and in other New England communities mill wheels were already turning to grid grain and saw lumber.

The settlers of Exeter wasted no time in granting land to Thomas Wilson in 1639 to build and operate his gristmill, located at the foot of the falls on the east side of the island formed by two channels of the river. Grinding by hand was much too time-consuming for the hewers of logs and builders of homes. A gristmill could free busy hands for more important tasks.

A gristmill's huge wheel had buckets attached to its rim. As the buckets filled at the top, the weight of the water carried the wheel around, turning two large, flat stones, one on top of the other. Corn or grain sifted down between the stones, and was ground into meal. A miller received part of the grain as payment, or was sometimes paid in beaver or otter skins. For the first time in the river's long history, it was lending its resource to be more than a travel route or a source of food and water.

Great as was the need for fish and grain, the products of surrounding forest were of equal importance to this growing village. Wood was the only available material for cabins, furniture, and even dishes. Pitch and turpentine were needed for building, and charcoal for fuel. Canoes and other "boats of burden" must be built to carry fish and furs to the Portsmouth market in exchange for staples and manufactured goods.

In a slow and laborious process called pit sawing, logs were cut with a two-handled saw, with one man standing below the log placed over a pit, the other above. The two men changed places at intervals, since the one at the lower level had to endure both heat and a shower of sawdust. So much manpower was used in pit sawing there was little time left for planting, fishing, hunting, and the processing of foods. A sawmill would be able to produce lumber five times faster.

In 1647, Edward Gilman came to Exeter from Hingham,

Massachusetts, perhaps for the very purpose of relieving this situation. Within a short time, he had been granted enough land to build Exeter's first sawmill on the west side of the river on the upper (higher) falls, along with enough woodland to furnish its materials. It is possible that he was assisted in the construction of the mill by James Wall, a signer of the Exeter deed, who had been sent by John Mason to the Dover area in 1634 to build sawmills.

Although the forest was already beginning to recede because of the onslaughts of the settlers, hemlock, spruce, and pine trees were still abundant. It was obvious, almost from the first, that a principal cash crop of the settlers had to be lumber. According to William Cronon in *Changes in the Land*, the Pilgrims had set the example by sending a load of clapboards to England on the first ship to leave Plymouth in 1621.

The thick forest surrounding Exeter, and a navigable river, insured a profitable business in wood products such as barrel staves, boards, shingles, and of course, masts. The lumber trade was to bring prosperity to the area for 100 years. It was probably Edward Gilman who built the first dam above the falls, using heavy timbers, rock, and packed earth to control the flow of water to give more power for milling.

The sawmill of those early days was a long, narrow, shingled building open at the ends to accommodate the logs that were sliced into lumber by saws that oscillated up and down. The saw was lifted up by the spring-like action of a timber pole and pulled down by the waterwheel crank cutting on the downstroke. Blacksmiths usually set up shop near the mills to forge iron machinery that quickly replaced the wooden parts first used.

Between 1650 and 1651, Gilman's mill produced 80,000 boards and planks. Soon ships built in Exeter and Newfields were carrying tons of wood products south to Virginia, to the West Indies, and even across the Atlantic, bringing back whale oil, rum, sugar, cloth, molasses, and manufactured goods.

"In the 1660s," Charles Clark wrote in *The Eastern Frontier*, "several mills were in operation along the Exeter and Squamscott Rivers." Among those mills would have been that of Humphrey Wilson, son of Thomas, whose sawmill was built on the east side of the river, and Edward Gilman's second sawmill on the west bank.

Farther upriver, the Reverend Samuel Dudley and John Legat built a sawmill at Pickpocket Falls. Their 1652 deed states that they were granted rights on the "second or third falls above the town on the fresh

Pickpocket Falls. Photo courtesy of J. Tardiff.

river." It was so far from the center of town that the mill was frequently raided by Indians. The Gilman Garrison House, built about 1675 near Great Bridge, was intended to provide protection against such incursions. Perhaps because of its existence, buildings near Great Falls were never attacked.

The Indians threat was not enough to keep Robert Seward and Thomas Crawley from building a sawmill in 1652 at what is now known as Crawley's Falls in Brentwood, a millsite whose waterpower was in use well into the 19th century.

There were some unavoidable problems in using the river as a source of power. During dry seasons, the water flow dropped too low to turn mill wheels. In winter, a thick ice cover could have the same effect. The "icing" of outside mill wheels sometimes closed down a unit for days. Larger dams could usually hold back enough water for later use; but small dams, which proliferated all the way to Chester, could not. Dams were often subject to damage from spring floods, when whole sections might be washed away.

In *Common Landscape of America*, John Stilgoe wrote, "Sawmilling civilized the land." The lumber business not only brought wealth to the

Basset's Mill, Fremont c. 1895. Matthew E. Thomas Collection.

settlers, but, Stilgoe asserted, the thinning out of forest made it easier to repel wild animals, Indians, and even French soldiers. And as more land was cleared, agriculture became simpler.

Not everyone was happy to see lumbering prosper. Judge Samuel Tenney, a leading Exeter citizen, writing in 1795, deplored lumbering as the "worst of all employments, ruining morals and inducing premature old age." He denounced the "low class, foreign" laborers who were attracted by the industry to the Exeter area, and complained that taverns were "thronged" with people every night.

Even as early as 1715, the town fathers had found it necessary to limit to two the number of taverns in Exeter. "It's a dissolute business," wrote Timothy Dwight after his visit to Exeter in 1796. "It is carried on by poor, idle haunters of taverns."

Although few in that era were aware of the ecological consequences of the destruction of the forests, Tenney did warn that dams were reducing the supply of shad, alewives, and salmon that could no longer swim upstream unimpeded. With a prospering economy, citizens apparently turned a deaf ear to Tenney's criticisms.

It is true that 100 years earlier, the town government had recognized the need for regulating the cutting of trees within the community, but that was more a means of preventing litigation between citizens than of preserving forests. In 1657, "range-ways" were created, reserving a two-mile strip of land in the west end of Exeter "for perpetual commage." This common land encompassed most of present-day Fremont. Ten acres of land were granted to those who qualified, with the understanding that enough timber would be left for masts, fence-building, and for boats. Not until 1754 was it found necessary to set limits on dams and seines so that one miller's use of the river did not interfere with another's.

The lumber industry was not the only villain in the continuing deforestation. Huge quantities of potash (used for fertilizer) and charcoal (fuel for iron furnaces) were produced, with one acre of hardwood forest needed for every two tons of potash. Colonists were burning four-and five-foot logs day and night in their fireplaces. The concept of conservation and selective cutting was centuries away.

Sometimes it seems as if every ripple in a stream was excuse enough to build a mill of some kind. An undershot wheel could be turned even by a brook to grind corn. A sawmill, with its typical overshot wheel, perhaps fifteen feet high and four feet wide, demanded more power. But that could be provided by a waterfall of only about eight feet, often furnished by a stream dammed up to form a holding pond. Samuel Tenney, in his 1795 essay, referred to the two dams "thrown" over the falls on the Great River.

In the early 1700s, mills were springing up all along the Exeter River. Even in the Squamscott, a tidemill, using water from tidal flats as they drained into Norris Creek (near Salem Street), was set up to grind bark for tanning.

The Black Rocks Mills, in Fremont (originally called Poplin), were built on both sides of the river to serve as grist- and sawmills, later producing woolens and wood products. About the same time, Daniel Ladd founded the Cavil Mill (later known as Caverley, Bassett, Brown's, or Scribner's) on one side of the Exeter River in Fremont. On the other bank, the Co-operative Mill was built by Alexander Magoon and 11 others, with each man to have one month's profits from the operation. Since the setting up of a mill and its equipment was expensive, such co-operative investments were common.

Among the *Accounts of Exeter, 1750-1800*, edited in 1938 by Howard T. Easton and William G. Saltonstall, are those of Joseph Hadfield, who traveled in this area in 1785, and the Duke of Rochefoucault, here in 1796. Both men noted in their journals that Exeter had several sawmills, gristmills, oil mills, and an ironworks. President George Washington, in his tour of New England in 1789, was impressed enough to comment on Exeter's "considerable falls" and its mills. Writing in 1796, Timothy Dwight further included two chocolate mills, two fulling mills, one paper mill, a snuff mill, and a nail-slitting mill.

Tobacco may have been ground into snuff and cacao beans into chocolate in much the same fashion that grain was ground into flour. Oil mills used grindstones to grind flaxseed, which had first been heated in a large kettle. As the linseed oil was released, its residue of crushed seed was then pressed into cakes for cattle feed. The nail-slitting process, invented in 1786, used machinery to slice and flatten iron bars into strips called nail rods, out of which pointed, headed nails could be forged. The old, slow method of forging nails by hand at a rural fireside gradually became obsolete.

Paper was made exclusively of rags. So essential was paper to the economy of the provincial government of New Hampshire that in 1777 Richard Jordan was given a loan of $200 to build a paper mill in Exeter at Pickpocket Falls. Moreover, the government asked town officers in various communities to advertise for rags. In the papermaking process a water-driven drum, armed with sharp spikes, rotated, and tore the rags into shreds. The resulting pulp was then spread on shallow trays, and the water drained off. The pulp was then pressed between two layers of felt and hung up to dry

The paper mill built by Jordan at Pickpocket Falls changed hands several times, and finally was owned by Thomas Wiswall and Isaac Flagg. Fire appears to have been a constant threat to the mills along the river, and Wiswall and Flagg's was no exception. Twice it had to be rebuilt after disastrous fires, and went out of business entirely in 1870.

Even more serious was the danger of explosion in the powder mill established at King's Falls in Exeter, near present-day Powdermill Road. Gunpowder was in such short supply when the Revolution began that, in 1776, Samuel Folsom of Exeter received from the Provincial Congress a loan of 300 pounds to seek out a "suitable person" to start a factory. Within two months, Colonel Samuel Hobart of Hollis had moved into the area and had a gunpowder operation underway.

Hobart's mill, known as the King's Falls Powder Company, used waterpower to pound, grind, and sift a mixture of saltpeter, sulfur, and charcoal, to produce about 2400 pounds of gunpowder a day. Some of that powder was stored for safety in the powderhouse built in 1771 on the

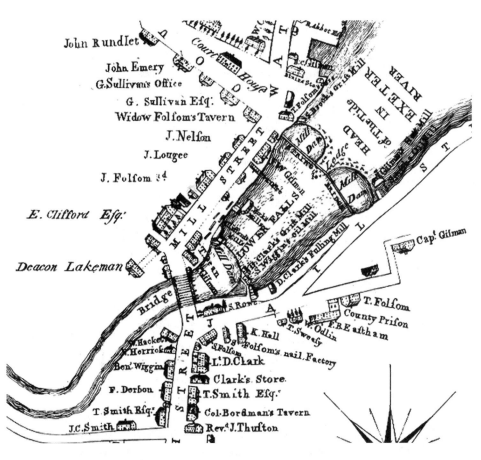

Phinehas Merrill's Map, 1802 Map courtesy of Exeter Historical Society.

east bank of the Squamscott. That sturdy building was ready to receive the gunpowder stolen from Fort William and Mary in Portsmouth in 1774. The recently renovated landmark stands on what is now known as Powderhouse Point as a reminder of the Squamscott's role in the Revolution.

Within a few years, Hobart sold his interest in the powder mill, and by 1785 was operating a nail-slitting mill. Part of the powder mill property was used after 1797 by Joshua Barstow for a gun factory.

It was fortunate that the powder mill had been built in an isolated spot, since it burned once, and was blown up three times. The last explosion in 1850 resulted in one fatality. Following that tragedy, the mill's last owner, Oliver Whipple, ceased the manufacture of gun powder. In 1855, Whipple sold his property to an Exeter resident, William H. Hunnewell, who then began the manufacture of hubs, spokes, and shingles.

The first reliable map of Exeter, drawn by Phinehas Merrill in 1802, shows the town considerably reduced in size by the formation of new villages: Newmarket in 1727 (part of which later became South Newmarket, then was renamed Newfields; Epping in 1741; Brentwood in 1742; and Poplin (later Fremont) in 1764. On his map, Merrill placed nine mills near Great Falls with the large mill dam near Great Bridge and two smaller wooden dams below at String Bridge, so called because at first it was merely a single log laid on rope cables.

The names of some of the 1802 mill owners are familiar ones even today: Gilman, Wiggin, Clark, and York. Changes had occurred since the observations of travelers in the late 1700s. Fires and floods had taken their toll; certain mill products had gone out of fashion.

While grist-and sawmills were still very much in evidence, the chocolate and snuff factories mentioned by Timothy Dwight do not appear on Merrilll's map. Nor is there any evidence that the ironworks apparently built at Crawley's Falls in 1750 was still operating. Bog iron, raked out of shallow ponds mostly in the Dover area, was never wholly satisfactory for use in making farm implements and other tools.

Two completely new industries were about to make their appearance on the Exeter River. In 1824, an enterprising young doctor, William Perry, started a potato-starch factory, using a formula of his own invention. Dr. Perry's factory, located on the east side of the river, was soon using about 35,000 bushels of potatoes per year to produce a starch that was considered by textile factory owners in Lowell to be superior to the British product they had been using.

It was said that the streets of Exeter were "lined with oxcarts" in the fall with loads of potatoes. Unfortunately, the potato-starch factory was burned to the ground twice (each time rebuilt), once in 1827 and again in 1830. Soon afterward, Dr. Perry was forced out of business when his starch formula was stolen by competitors.

Never were the demands on the Exeter River greater than when it was called upon to provide power for the Exeter Manufacturing Company's cotton mill. The first water-powered cotton mill in the United States had been operated by Samuel Slater in Pawtucket, Rhode Island, since 1790. "Spinning and weaving," wrote Ben Bachman in *Upstream,* "consist of a few simple motions repeated over and over again…and could be done at

Putting the River to Work

Exeter Manufacturing Co. Photo courtesy of Exeter Historical Society.

high speed with the help of falling water." Businessmen in Massachusetts and New Hampshire who saw its potential were quick to take up this new industry.

The Exeter River was already supplying power for two textile mills – Nicholas Gilman's woolen mill, built in 1803, and Benjamin Hoitt's 1815 Rockingham Cotton Manufactory, located at Pickpocket Falls. These must have been small enterprises compared to the one soon to begin on the east bank of the Squamscott.

The population of Exeter was about 2500 in 1827, the year that Nathaniel Gilman, John Taylor Gilman, Bradbury Cilley, Steven Hanson, John Rogers, Nathaniel Gilman, 3rd, and Paine Wingate formed a corporation known as the Exeter Manufacturing Company. In 1828, the company took control of the Exeter Mill and Water Power Company, already set up to provide the mill with power. Among the many prominent stockholders of the new company was Daniel Webster.

Constructed with timber from New Hampshire forest and with locally baked brick, the main three-story building was ready in 1830 to begin producing its first yard of cotton cloth. Its 175 Scotch looms and 5000 spindles were operated at first mainly by local workers. The recently invented power loom made it possible for whole families to be employed. Men ran the looms and did other heavy tasks, women did the spinning, and children as young as nine years of age tended machinery, picked off lint, and tied broken threads. New mothers kept their babies in baskets at their sides while they worked.

The Exeter Manufacturing Company gradually bought out all the mills that appeared on Merrill's 1802 map, so that no water would be diverted for other uses. Even under the best conditions, the company could develop only 320 horsepower; during the dry season, it produced far less. The supply of water may have been of concern from the very first, since in 1831 a survey of the river was authorized by the company. The surveyor was instructed to make recommendations for increasing the flow of water to the mill.

In that survey, taken from Exeter's Great Falls to the river's source in Chester, 12 mills, including Wiswall and Flagg's paper mill, Robinson's Crawley's, Copyhold, Gibson's and Clark's sawmills, and eight dams were identified. The surveyor recommended such measures as creating a reservoir at

Logo of Flag and Wiswall. Courtesy of Howard Easton.

Phillips Pond in Sandown, widening and straightening the Exeter River, or raising the dam in Exeter. None of these actions was apparently ever taken. Probably the mill simply shut down during the dry seasons. Not until 1876 would the power supplied by its four 36-inch water wheels be supplemented by a stationary steam engine.

The Exeter Manufacturing Company not only affected the economy of the area by providing a stable base of employment and taxes, but also changed the ethnic character of the town. Entire families migrated from Ireland, England, and Germany, and later from Canada to seek work at the mill.

The original "mill girls" from farm homes had boarded locally during the week and returned to their families on Sunday. With the influx of new employees, attracted by wages averaging from $2 to $8 per week depending on the type of work, it became necessary for owners of the mill to build housing near the factory. Tenements along the river rented for about $5 a month, and double-family homes for more, but single family houses were generally reserved for supervisory personnel.

A 1974 map of Exeter shows a tenement (typically two stories with four apartments of six rooms) on the site of Dr. Perry's potato starch factory, and a similar building on the corner of Franklin and Water Streets, now the restored "Long Block."

The Squamscott River was pressed into service, carrying the barges that brought bales of raw cotton from the South, and taking rolls of finished cotton sheeting to Portsmouth for trans-shipment to other ports. Its waters, too, took away effluents from the mill. Chemicals and dyes entered a river already unfortunately polluted by raw sewage from outhouses and from two town sewer lines that emptied directly into it. Had it not been for the scouring action of the tide, downtown Exeter would have been an impossible place to live and work.

At the turn of the 20th century, with George Kent at the helm, the Exeter Manufacturing Company was using 5000 bales of cotton, and its 300 workers were producing 7,000,000 yards of cloth each year.

Under the management of three generations of the Kent family (Hervey, his son George, and grandson Hervey), the mill prospered. It continued to operate on a reduced scale even during the Depression of the 1930s, and made a strong comeback in World War II. By the middle of the 20th century, however, it became apparent that northern cotton mills could no longer compete with the lower costs of production in the South. In 1955, the last yard of cotton was woven in Exeter. Three hundred fifty looms were broken up and taken away to be replaced by machinery to make synthetic materials.

In 1966, the Exeter Manufacturing Company was sold to Milliken Industrials, Inc. which continued the production of synthetic materials. Milliken's business declined, and in 1980 the Exeter-Squamscott River's last textile mill was purchased by Nike, a manufacturer of running-shoes. Nike ceased production in Exeter in 1984. Today the mill lies idle, waiting for its next assignment.

Over the years, mills along the river have changed ownership many times, with new methods and products introduced to meet public demands. Profitable businesses were carried on particularly in Brentwood and Fremont in the 19th and early 20th centuries, producing wheelbarrows, buggies, carriages, wheels, spokes, furniture, shoe boxes, washing machines, clapboards, and shingles. Many mills burned down, and were often rebuilt. Sometimes dams, bridges, and buildings were washed out by spring floods. Especially disastrous were the floods of 1927 and 1936 which wiped out some mill operations on the upper river front.

Only two working mills remain to serve as reminders of a busy past. At Turner's Mills, on the site of the Co-operative and Cavil Mills in Fremont, plastic products are being made with electric-powered machinery. Near Copyhold Bridge in West Brentwood, the last water-powered mill on the entire river supplies hydropower to 24 families using an oil-fired generator during dry seasons.

Meanwhile the Exeter-Squamscott River flows on, diverted only for minimal power, less sullied today by man-made pollutants. Thanks to environmental protection laws passed in recent decades, the river above and below the falls has been restored to a condition unknown since mills began to crowd its banks in the 17th century.

Mills on the Exeter River 1639-1900

1639	Thomas Wilson	Gristmill	Exeter
1648	Edward Gilman, Jr.	Sawmill	West bank, Exeter
1650	Edward Gilman, Jr.	Sawmill	East bank, Exeter
ca.1650	John Gilman	Gristmill	West bank, Exeter
ca.1650	Humphrey Wilson & others	Sawmill	East bank, Exeter
1652	Rev. Samuel Dudley	Sawmill	Pickpocket Falls
	John Legat		Exeter
1652	Robert Seward,	Sawmill	Crawley's Falls
	Thomas Crawley	Brentwood	
1657	Edward Hilton, Jr.	Sawmill	Exeter
ca. 1700	Black Rocks Mills	Sawmill & gristmill	Fremont
ca. 1700	Copyhold Mill	Sawmill	W. Brentwood
	(John Gilman?)		
ca. 1700	Alexander Magoon	Sawmill & gristmill	Both sides of river, Fremont
	11 others, Cavil Mills, Co-operative Mill		

1720	Col. Packer & others	Sawmill	Chester
1730	John Aiken	Sawmill & gristmill	Upper & lower falls, Chester
1741	James Campbell Daniel McDuffee	Sawmill & gristmill	Chester
1748	William Graves Delicate or Dilicutt Mill	Sawmill	Brentwood
ca. 1750	Zaccheus Clough	Sawmill	Fremont
1750	Sawmill	Crawley's Falls	Brentwood
1751	Theophilus Sargent, & others	Sawmill	Chester
1756	Samuel Gibson (Shirking or Sherkend Mill)	Sawmill	Brentwood
1757	Ironworks	Crawley's Falls	Brentwood
1765	John Scribner (Cavil Mills)	Gristmill	Fremont
ca. 1760	Merrymeeting Mill (1767, Fuller's)	Sawmill	Sandown
1768	James Merrill	Sawmill	Black Rocks, Fremont
1771	Robert Wilson	Sawmill	Chester
1776	Col. Samuel Hobart	Powdermill	King's Falls, Exeter
1777	Richard Jordan	Papermill	King's Falls, Exeter
1780	Capt. William Lock & others	Sawmill	Chester
1780	Clark's Mill (Formerly Fuller's)	Sawmill & gristmill	Sandown
1785	Col. Samuel Hobart	Nail-slitting	Exeter
1787	Eliphalet Hale (Formerly Jordan's)	Paper mill	Exeter
1797	Joshua Barstow (Formerly Hobart's)	Gun factory	Exeter
ca. 1800	Hazleton's Mill	Shingle & clapboard	Chester
1800	Currier	Sawmill	Sandown
ca. 1800	Stephen Sleeper	Sawmill	Fremont
1802	Phinehas Merrill's map	Mills in Exeter	
	E. Clifford	Gristmill & sawmill	West bank
	D. York	Gristmill & sawmill	West bank
	D. Clark	Gristmill & fulling mill	East bank
	S. Gilman	Sawmill	East bank
	J. Smith	Oil mill	East bank

	S. Brock	Gristmill	West bank
1803	Nicholas Gilman	Woolen mill	Exeter
1808	John Locke & others	Sawmill	Chester
1815	Benjamin Hoitt	Cotton Mill	Pickpocket Falls
	Rockingham Manufactory		Exeter
1815	Thomas Wiswall &	Paper Mill	King's Falls, Exeter
	Isaac Flagg		
1820	John Locke	Corn Mill	Chester
1824	Dr. William Perry	Potato Starch	Exeter
1830	Exeter Manufacturing Co.	Cotton	Exeter
1835	William Swett	Gunpowder	King's Falls, Exeter
	King's Falls Powder Co.		
1841	Oliver Whipple	Gunpowder	King's Falls, Exeter
ca. 1850	Andrew George	Cooperage & sawmill	Sandown
1850-80	Co-operative Mill	Furniture	Fremont
1851	Union Paper Mill	Also Corn & gristmill	Union Village Brentwood
1855	Edwin Morrill		Crawley's Falls Brentwood
1855	William Hunnewell	Gristmill & sawmill	Exeter
1862	John Fellows	Box mill	W. Brentwood
1875	Whittier Bros.	Shoe boxes, etc.	Black Rocks Fremont

Survey of Exeter River, above dam, 1831
By Exeter Manufacturing Company

Mills & dams on Exeter River
Exeter, both dams (upper & lower)
Rockingham Factory
Wiswall & Flagg's Paper Mill
Pickpocket dam
Robinson's Mills
Crawley's Mills & dams
Morrill's dams
Copyhold Mills (two dams)
Scribner's (Graves & others)
Gibson's Mill
Lock & True's dam
Crawford's Mill dam
Clark's Mills

Mills Listed in "Accounts of Exeter" – 1750-1800
(Easton & Saltonstall, 1938)
10 gristmills
1 paper mill
1 fulling mill
1 slitting mill
1 snuff mill
2 chocolate mills
6 sawmills
1 tobacco factory
2 oil mills
1 ironworks

CHAPTER III

☙

THE MAST TRADE

England could hardly wait for New England to be settled. Over the centuries, forests in the British Isles had been stripped to meet the constant demand for building materials and firewood. Many colonists are said to have left England because of the shortage of fuel. With Britain's sea trade increasing, there was an especially desperate need for ships masts.

In 1620, English explorers had mapped the New England coast, and brought back word of the huge pines that grew along northern shores. The supply of Norwegian masts, England's chief source, was dropping, and the heavily forested colonies were eyed hopefully.

As early as 1652, while the colonists were struggling to get a foothold in the New World, the King of England sent men to mark with his "Broad Arrow" (shaped like a crow's track) all pines suitable for masts. The largest and finest growth of the forest was reserved for the King, a practice that became a standing grievance to the colonists. They believed this to be an encroachment on open land, and felt it was not morally wrong to thwart the emissaries of the Royal Navy who came to supervise the collection of masts.

Sometimes men cut down smaller trees surrounding the majestic pines, hoping that as a tree crashed to the ground without its cushion of brush, it would crack and become unfit for use as a mast. The broken trunk could then be chopped up or sawed into lumber for local use. Pines, hemlocks, and spruce were valued not only for lumber, but for tar, pitch, and turpentine, and for bark for tanning leather. It was no wonder that ways were found to keep the timber for private use. A potential mast tree might be secretly cut down and carried off to a nearby sawmill. The sharp eyes of the surveyors for the Crown often detected these ruses, and there were frequent clashes with the colonists.

Lumbering Camp in Winter, 1882. New Hampshire Historical Society.

In 1721, an act of Parliament forbade the cutting of any white pine growing outside of a township, further antagonizing New Englanders whose demand for their own ships' masts and timbers was increasing. The Mast Tree Riot of 1734 occurred when a group of Exeter residents, dressed like Indians, frightened away the men sent by Surveyor-General David Dunbar of Portsmouth to check on all white pine boards sawed from mast trees and taken to mills along the Exeter River.

The mast trade was profitable mainly to the agents who located and claimed the trees, and to those who transported them by ship. For the "cruisers," who cut, trimmed and hauled masts to waiting ships, it was hard work at low pay.

The giant pines sometimes weighing as much as 18 tons were felled by axes. Care had to be taken that they would land on layers of smaller trees, or, in winter, on piles of snow. Once a tree was cut down, its branches were removed, it was trimmed, cut to the proper size, and stripped of its bark. The most desirable masts averaged 35 inches in diameter and were about 200 feet long. Because of the dense growth around them, they were often free of sprouting limbs for the first 80 feet from the bottom. The finest specimens were worth about $500, a considerable sum in those days.

Winter was the best time for the laborious task of dragging the mast tree to the riverside. Logs could be rolled onto sledges and pulled by teams of oxen, then slid down to the frozen river. There the logs would remain until spring, when they could be floated downriver to mast-houses where mastwrights smoothed and tapered the tree trunks into a 16-sided spar before loading them onto ships.

Jeremy Belknap, 18th century New Hampshire historian wrote, "When a mast is to be drawn, as its length will not permit of its passing in a crooked road, a straight path is cut and cleared for it through the woods." Almost every town had its "Mast Road," connecting stands of pine with the river. "Ye old mast way," mentioned in Exeter records, ran along Park Street (then called Back Street) to Lane's End, where logs were unloaded and rolled down a steep bank in the water.

When masts were transported in summer, they were slung in heavy chains below two axles, each connecting a pair of enormous wheels that could go over rocks, stumps, and gullies. In a record shipment, it is reported that 100 pairs of oxen were used, 32 at the front of the load, 8 at the sides, and the remaining ones at the rear, with one man guiding each yoke of oxen.

On descending a steep hill, the brakes (or drogues) could not always hold the entire moving mass, and some oxen might be crushed by those in back of them as they were thrown forward. As the team of oxen reached the crest of a hill, the forward pairs were sometimes suspended in the air by the weight of the rear load. Any disabled oxen were then cut out of the string, and fresh pairs yoked into place.

A mast ship might wait weeks for a load to arrive. Ships remained tied up at wharves built on the Squamscott for the convenience of upriver merchants. Some ships were large enough to sail directly across the Atlantic, but more often the masts were transferred to large vessels in Portsmouth Harbor, to set sail for England, Mediterranean countries, and even Africa and the Orient. A good sized ship of 400- to 600-ton capacity could carry 45 or 50 large masts per voyage, and a few passengers as well. In 1671, 10 such cargoes of masts, many perhaps from Exeter forests, left Portsmouth, bound for England.

From 1712 to 1718, England got 638 large, 262 medium, and 88 small masts from the Piscataqua region. In *Ports of Piscataqua*, William G.

Saltonstall cited a letter of 1715 stating that "every winter great numbers of men and teams, chiefly from Exeter [are] sent up into the woods…where they cut 1500 large pine trees and hall them in loggs into the river."

The mast trade caused problems in local river travel. Although a bridge may have been built as early as 1644 over the Exeter River, teamsters usually forded the Squamscott at low tide, while foot and horse travelers paid a small fee to cross by ferry. But the ferry could not be used during the spring break-up of ice.

In 1746, Newfields residents petitioned the state for a drawbridge to replace the ferry. Exeter residents objected, claiming that a bridge would restrict fishing, and that ships carrying masts and timber would be more difficult to handle in tidal waters when obstructed by a bridge. The "Lottery Bridge" (so called because money for it was raised by a lottery) was finally built in 1775. By that time the mast trade had begun to decline.

For some time, the supply of masts had been dwindling. As early as 1750, James Birket, merchant and sea captain from Antigua, reported after a visit to Exeter that "lumber was far to fetch and very dear," and that it was necessary to go more than 20 miles from town to find suitable trees. As nearby forests were denuded, the mast trade gradually moved northeastward, with Falmouth (Portland), Maine, instead of Portsmouth, becoming its center. A prosperous trade, but one that had severely depleted Exeter's surrounding forest, had ended.

๛

CHAPTER IV

SHIPBUILDING ON THE SQUAMSCOTT

To look at the tranquil Squamscott River today, its main channel at lowest tide a mere trickle of water, we can hardly imagine it as a busy inland port. Yet Charles Bell reported that in the middle of the 18th century, ship and lumber yards "stretched almost continuously between stores and wharves from the lower falls to meeting house hill." In his 1888 history, Bell wrote that the remains of the old shipyards (perhaps those of Peter Coffin or John and Peter Gilman) were still visible at very low tide.

From the building of the first ship, Edward Gilman's 50-ton vessel, in 1651, to the launching of the 400-ton *Nile* in Newfields in 1825, the west bank of the Squamscott was a busy scene. Portsmouth harbor, about 25 miles downriver from Exeter's Great Falls, was said to be one of the three best ports on the North Atlantic coast because of its depth and the strong currents that kept its waters open even in the dead of winter.

It was natural that Piscataqua tributaries with their nearby woodlands should foster shipbuilding, even though those inlets are generally described as being narrow, tortuous, and shallow. It was easier and cheaper to build near a supply of white oak than to float the lumber all the way to Portsmouth. The cost for building a ship on the Squamscott in the 1780s was less than $25 a ton.

The most important order of business for the first settlers of Exeter had been the building of boats for river transport. These were probably either heavy dugout canoes, similar to those of the Indians, or sturdy flatboats propelled by poles, used for fishing and for freighting cattle and produce between Portsmouth and Exeter. With dense forest stretching from Boston northward, the river, after all, was the main highway. No other form of transportation could be counted on.

In 1692, two 20-ton sloops built in Exeter, the *Elizabeth* and the *Endeavour*, were launched to travel downriver across Great Bay and Little Bay to the mouth of Portsmouth harbor, and from there to Boston. The *Elizabeth* is known to have carried a heavy burden of boards and barrel staves and to have returned with a lighter load of marsh hay from Hampton. It marked the beginning of a steady flow of river traffic that was to last almost 200 years, fluctuating with the fortunes of peace and war in the nation.

While tides normally permitted even 500-ton ships to float down the Squamscott to be fitted out with masts, spars, cordage, and sails in Portsmouth, the river's twists and turns made the return of such vessels impossible. This fact did not discourage the building of hulls for both local owners and others in Portsmouth, Philadelphia, New York and England.

Small sloops and schooners had difficulty enough getting through the Oxbow (about three miles below the falls), and often had to navigate its curves with the aid of their 40-foot poles or sweeps, or by throwing out small anchors ahead of the boat to draw it forward. As Saltonstall stated in his *Ports of Piscataqua*, "No wind could have been fickle enough to get a boat equipped with sails through the Great Roundabout." Sometimes it was necessary for a vessel to wait as long as a week for favorable winds and tides in order to reach Exeter.

Not all ships were built at the edge of the Squamscott. Saltonstall wrote that small sloops were sometimes built in marshy creeks, on flat meadows, or deep in the forest, perhaps as far inland as 15 or 20 miles. Matthew Thomas of Fremont reports finding in that town's record the names of Abijah Joy, caulker, 1775; Jonathan Coffin, shipwright, 1774; and Nathaniel Currier, shipwright, 1774—all ship's artisans presumably working near their Poplin (Fremont) homes.

Some ships built far from the Squamscott were hauled in winter by as many as 100 yokes of oxen to the frozen river, there to wait for launching with the coming of spring and open water. Sometimes a ship would be built in the woods, taken apart, its sections numbered, and re-assembled on the banks of the river. Such was the procedure with the *General Sullivan*, built in 1777 in Lee and hauled to Newmarket for launching.

By 1700, river trade was no longer simply a means of survival; it had become a thriving industry. "On the banks of the Squamscott," wrote

Bell, "from morning till night the sounds of the carpenter's adze and the calker's mallet…arose from the hulls propped up on the ways." Shipwrights, some of whom were Negroes, were allowed half an hour for breakfast, one hour for dinner, and received an average pay of $5 for a six-day week. They appeared to be satisfied with the wage as long as they got their daily grog and a special tot of rum "at the launch."

Other industries sprang up to meet the needs of shipbuilders. Chains, anchors, and other iron work for ships were hammered out at conveniently placed blacksmith shops. The earlier bog iron was replaced with iron of better quality imported from England.

On being promised a bounty from the New Hampshire Legislature of seven shillings for each bolt of canvas produced, Deacon Thomas Odiorne, in 1780, opened his Duck Manufactory in Exeter, the first in the state, and the only such mill in the Piscataqua district. Odiorne used linen yarn from locally grown flax, and employed 16 weavers and spinners to produce what was considered a fine quality of sailcloth.

Small coasting sloops, schooners, and an early type of gundalow were built mainly for regional trade. Although some Exeter-built ships of just 250 tons could cross the Atlantic, they more commonly headed for ports in the West Indies with cargoes of lumber, bricks, dried cod, and salted alewives. They brought back corn, hides, beef, pork, molasses, and rum to be dumped on the floor of Water Street stores whose entrances were on the Squamscott.

The height of shipbuilding activity in Exeter is variously set by historians. Bell claimed 1750-1775 as the "Great Era," pointing out that the industry declined during the Revolution and never fully recovered. Saltonstall described "increasing activity up the Piscataqua tributaries throughout the 18th century, and referred to the years between 1750 and 1760 as the "Golden period," when as many as 22 vessels were built in a single season.

Yet, in the 1780s, seven builders were at work in Exeter shipyards. Joseph Hadfield, after his 1785 visit, declared, "This is a great place for building ships. We saw a beautiful one on the stocks." (Perhaps it was the 75-ton schooner *Jane* built in that year.) George Washington saw 300- and 400-ton ships being built in 1789. Between 1791 and 1800, 21 ships were launched in Exeter.

The largest ship built on the Squamscott was the 498-ton *Hercules*, 112 feet long and 31 feet wide. It was built in 1793 for Eliphalet Ladd by

Eliphalet Giddinge (also spelled Giddings) and Ephraim Robinson at Robinson's wharf, which was located near the middle of present-day Swasey Parkway. The *Hercules* was so massive that it had to be buoyed up with empty hogsheads for its trip down the Squamscott. Because of its length, it appears to have been built parallel to the river and launched sideways. It met the fate of many ships of that period, captured by a British privateer and sold in Halifax in 1796.

One of the most active shipbuilders of Exeter was Joseph Swasey (also spelled Swazey) who is credited with building the first full-rigged ocean-going vessel to float downriver to Portsmouth, launched from his wharf at Lane's End. Swasey built nine ships between 1800 and 1807, but his total output was perhaps surpassed by Benjamin Conner, who, according to Bell, lived to be 101 years old and built 60 vessels during his lifetime.

Almost as busy were Eliphalet and Nathaniel Giddinge, and Eliphalet Ladd who moved to Portsmouth in 1792, but continued his investment in Exeter shipbuilding, owning a total of six ships. James Hackett of Exeter, a renowned master carpenter, was the builder of the 74-gun *America* in Portsmouth in 1784 under the supervision of John Paul Jones.

One of the most interesting stories told about Exeter ships concerns the 158-ton *Oliver Peabody*, built in 1799 by Samuel Chamberlain. This brig, owned by Governor John Gilman and others, and captained by Stephen Gilman, left Portsmouth in 1803 carrying a cargo of lumber and a deck load of oxen, sheep, and poultry. When about 20 days out of port, and approaching the Windward Islands, Capt. Gilman was shocked to find his ship surrounded by a sizable fleet of men-of-war which he at first took to be French.

To his surprise, he was invited to board the flagship, where he met Admiral Horatio Nelson of the British fleet. According to Brewster's *Rambles about Portsmouth*, Nelson "treated him with a glass of wine and great politeness." The admiral, it seems, was most interested in Capt. Gilman's cargo of livestock. To replenish the fleet's supply of meat, Nelson offered to buy the entire stock at the going rate.

The *Oliver Peabody* returned home to port with its usual load of trade goods, plus a triumphant Capt. Gilman bearing 10,000 Spanish dollars. In 1810, the *Oliver Peabody* met the fate of many ocean-going Piscataqua vessels and was lost at sea.

There is a fine line between piracy and privateering, and Exeter merchants were well acquainted with the latter practice. Too many crew members had lost their lives, too many fortunes had been forfeited, and too many men imprisoned far from home in the 18th century for them not to understand the procedure of capturing a ship, forcing its crew to sail to a friendly port, and disposing of its cargo to the advantage of the captors.

After receiving permission in 1776 from the New Hampshire Legislature to prey on British commerce, at least 100 privateers sailed out of Portsmouth with large crews that made it possible for them to commandeer enemy ships. Ownership of shares in privateering vessels entitled merchants to a percentage of the profits. Privateering was patriotic as well as profitable, but it was dangerous, too. The damage to British shipping was counterbalanced by the loss of American lives and the imprisonment of hundreds of New Hampshire seamen under appalling conditions.

Many Exeter investors, including such familiar names as Ladd, Robinson, Lamson, Hackett, Jewett, and Giddinge, profited handsomely from this period of privateering that lasted until the end of the Revolution in 1783.

It is easy to overlook the importance of Newfields (until 1727 part of Exeter) as a shipbuilding center. Portsmouth customs records do not separate Exeter-built ships from those launched at Newfields Landing, at the foot of the present Squamscott Street. George Norton may have built his first ship at that spot in 1667. Members of the Shute and Badger families were principal shipbuilders there in the 18th and early 19th centuries.

It was in Newfields that James Hill "got out" the lumber brought down from Lee for the warship *America*; and just across the river in Stratham, the 343-ton *Niagara* was built in 1811 by Samuel Dutch. A profitable direct trade was carried on between Newfields and the West Indies until the three-year blockade of the seacoast during the War of 1812.

The launching of the *Nile* in 1825 marked the last of shipbuilding in Newfields. The event was celebrated in gala fashion, with games, sociability, and refreshments. Newfields remained an important commercial center well into the 19th century. Ironically, the steel rails used in building the tracks for the Boston and Maine Railroad that was soon to replace much of the river trade, were delivered to the Landing by ships from Portsmouth.

Three-masted schooner on Squamscott River. Courtesy of Exeter Historical Society.

In the 1880s, Saltonstall reported, a three-masted coal schooner was frozen into the ice all winter in Newfields, "her crew taken part in the regular life of the town." It was certainly not the first severe winter to hamper shipping. Samuel Lane of Stratham noted in his *Journal* that the winter of 1762 was extremely cold. "Vessels began to come in about the middle of March," Lane wrote, and in 1780, "there was so much snow that people could not use roads, but had to travel on the river between Portsmouth and Exeter [presumably on ice] the greatest part of the way until the end of March." In 1848, according to Lane's *Journal*, there was a "tedious hard Cold and Most Difficult winter...Deep Snows...scarcely any passing in Roads, with great difficulty throu' fields, on Rivers."

At the end of its shipbuilding phase, in the 1830s, Newfields Landing was brought to life again, first with an iron foundry in 1830, then by the establishment of the Swampscott Machine Company in 1846. Taking advantage of the transportation provided by the railroad that passed along the riverbank, Amos Paul's company successfully produced steam engines and a variety of other machinery.

Both political and natural forces brought the glories of major shipbuilding on the Squamscott to an end. As woodlands diminished, lumbering moved northeastward and took with it ship's carpenters and artisans. Falmouth, Maine (Portland) replaced Portsmouth as a center for foreign commerce.

The Embargo Act of 1807 and the restrictions on shipping in the War of 1812 led to the decline in importance of the Piscataqua's river ports at Dover, Durham, and Exeter. A few more large ships were built after 1815, but the emphasis shifted to the more practical, less profitable river boat.

In the 19th century the gundalow, described by Howard J. Chapelle in *History of American Sailing Ships* as one of the distinctive and curious of American types," came into its own. Gundalows (various spellings) may have got their name from that equally unusual craft, the Venetian gondola, perhaps because they were propelled by 40-foot sweeps of oars and were able to carry heavy loads in shallow water. According to *New Hampshire Past and Present*, these barges were "a form of transportation found nowhere else in the world."

The gundalow represented the next stage of river transportation after the square-ended scows in use as early as 1659 in Portsmouth for carrying goods and passengers. Tides of six to eight feet in Piscataqua tributaries provided the principal power. Even after gundalows were fitted out, about 1800, with rudders, tillers, and a lateen (triangular) sail fastened to a ten-foot mast that could be lowered to "shoot the bridges," the motto of the gundalow operator was "down one tide, home the next." In some stretches of the Squamscott, especially at the Oxbow, it was necessary to set stakes along the banks to pull a heavily-laden gundalow upstream.

Henry Shute, Exeter's humorous writer, once described the gundalow as "flat-bottomed, with leg-of-mutton sail, pair of sweeps, 1/2 doz. push-poles, crew of three men, and jug of New England rum."

It was the 1808 sinking of a gundalow loaded with iron bars in 72 feet of water in the Piscataqua River that inspired the inventive genius of Ebenezer Clifford, resident of Exeter's Gilman Garrison at the time. According to an account by Exeter historian Herbert C. Varney, Clifford devised a diving bell almost six feet high and five feet across that carried two tons of 56-pound iron weights, and held seats for two passengers.

Clifford is said to have made many successful descents in his diving bell, apparently recovering about half the iron bars. Although he was later

Gundalow with wood. Courtesy of Exeter Historical Society.

sued by Richard Tripe of Dover who felt he had first claim on the salvaged iron, Clifford won the case, and earned about $2,500 for his efforts. Clifford claimed that his dives below the surface of the Piscataqua improved his chronic rheumatism. The wooden swan float used for communication between the diver and the salvage ship above the surface is still displayed at the Gilman Garrison House.

Gundalows of about 5 to 10 tons capacity and 50 feet long linked inland communities with coastal and trans-Atlantic trade. Farmers from northern New Hampshire brought their produce in drays to Exeter wharves, then returned home with manufactured goods transshipped in Portsmouth from sea-going vessels. By the 1890s at least 25 of these utility boats were operating in the Piscataqua basin.

The Squamscott gundalows did a brisk business transporting bricks, flour, salt, coal, lumber, and alewives. For many years they carried bales of raw cotton to the Exeter Manufacturing Company, then returned to Portsmouth with finished cloth. After the railroad came to Exeter in 1840, cotton products were more often taken to and from the Boston and Maine station by horse drawn wagons in summer, and by sledges in winter.

The *Alice*, *News–Letter*, and *Red Jacket*, built in the 1870s by Joseph Furnald (also spelled Fernald) had a market value of about $1500. They carried cordwood, hay, stone, and coal, as well as an occasional passenger. Furnald had bought Ephraim Robinson's old wharf and had begun a gundalow service that was later taken over by his son George.

Saltonstall reported that it was not uncommon for a gundalow to leave Exeter at sunrise with "an ebbing tide and following wind," arrive in Portsmouth to unload about noon, reload, and come upriver "on a rising tide with a northeast wind," and reach Exeter just before dark. "The record time from Newmarket landing to Portsmouth and return was 6¼ hours!" wrote Saltonstall.

Two attempts have been made in recent years to keep the tradition of the gundalow alive. In 1950, on his 90th birthday, Captain Edward Adams of Durham launched the scaled-down gundalow *Driftwood*, built with the help of his son, Cass, over a period of 20 years. The *Driftwood* followed the design of Adams' last working gundalow, the *Fannie M.*, launched in 1886.

Although unfortunately the *Driftwood* was burned by vandals in 1970, that was not the end of the gundalow story. On June 13, 1982, the *Captain Edward H. Adams*, a modern replica of the *Fannie M.* was launched on the Piscataqua River. It then proceeded, as planned, up the Oyster River to arrive in time for the celebration of the 250th anniversary of the founding of Durham.

That project, which lasted six years, cost $100,000 and required enormous energy and inventiveness. Its initiator was Albert E. Hickey, who secured the help of the University of New Hampshire to build the vessel at Strawbery Banke, working from the original plans of the *Fannie M.*. Some of the special timbers needed for its construction came from the same Fremont woods that had produced lumber for shipbuilding in the 18th and 19th centuries. At present, the *Captain Adams* is on display in Portsmouth off Prescott Park, a picturesque reminder of the days of what Richard E. Winslow has called the "workhorse of the tidal basin."

The story of Squamscott shipping would not be complete without mention of the useful keel boats known as packets that operated in these waters until about 1870. Most of these 30-foot vessels of about 15 tons, handled by a two-man crew, were owned by Joseph Furnald. In Saltonstall's words, they carried "upstate goods to large ships in the Portsmouth harbor, and returned with exciting goods from the West Indies, Spain, England, Russia or the Orient."

Like the gundalow, the packet had a lateen sail that could be lowered for passage under bridges. Cargo was carried below decks, passengers above. Furnald's packets made about one or two round trips each week between Great Falls (Exeter) and Ladd's wharf (Portsmouth), for about 12 1/2 cents per person. Enough food was taken along to provide for the passengers in case the trip was delayed by unfavorable tides, sometimes as long as 24 hours. Pleasure trips on packets sometimes included a sail to the Isles of Shoals, leaving Exeter at 9 A.M. and reaching the Isles about 2 P.M.

With the advent of steam power, the Squamscott took on a less romantic appearance. Coal to stoke boilers of the Exeter Manufacturing Company and PEA was brought upriver by Henry Anderson's tug-propelled schooners that tied up at his wharf near the entrance of the present Swasey Parkway. In that same location, Albert W. McReel and others carried on successful coal businesses until oil supplanted coal for general heating in Exeter homes, schools, and industries. In early days, the coal was delivered by boat to the wharves, then hoisted to the coal-yards with power provided by donkeys or horses. Later an engine performed the same function.

The ever-narrowing Squamscott, filled in with silt that washed over the falls, and thickening with mud sliding from its banks, was a constant problem for shipping of all kinds. When Congress voted $20,000 in 1880 for the first dredging of the river, it was agreed that the Oxbow should be cut through at the same time. Many a gundalow or barge had foundered in the curves of the Oxbow. Loads of granite blocks had to be carted to the river below the Oxbow to be sent downriver to Portsmouth, thus avoiding entrapment in the "Great Roundabout."

Only 15 years after that dredging, a complaint in the *Exeter News-Letter* of October 4, 1896 cited the need for a channel of a depth of nine feet at high tide since vessels were frequently grounded. "It is important," the article stated, "to have the channel extended to the wharves for coal traffic." Again in 1903, dredging took place, but did not solve the problem for long.

In a survey of 1910, the U.S. Army Corps of Engineers found the annual total commerce on the river to be 10,000 tons, mostly of coal, but including lumber, cordwood, and fish. Schooners *Lizzie J. Call*, *Ada J. Campbell*, and *Florence A.*, transporting coal directly from New York, could carry only 90% capacity because of the silted-in condition of the Squamscott. No river traffic at all was carried on for four months in winter.

Dredged again in 1911, the channel reached the desirable standard of 11 to 12 feet deep, 40 feet wide, with a broad turning basin near the foot of the falls. A serious handicap to shipping was the Newfields-Stratham drawbridge, built at such an inconvenient angle that ships had to turn sharply in cross currents to get through. For a number of years, the Corps of Engineers' 1910 report stated, conditions there were the cause of complaint and litigation.

By the time the Swasey Parkway was under construction in 1930, it was necessary again to widen and deepen the channel, this time financed with funds from Ambrose Swasey and from PEA. Currently, in 1986, sentiment is growing for yet another dredging to enhance the beauty of the river and to make downtown Exeter, with its new emphasis on river-front development, a haven for pleasure boats.

The end of Squamscott River shipbuilding came with the launching of the coal barge *Merrill*, owned by Henry Anderson, in 1902. It was the occasion of a great celebration by townspeople. Helen Tufts Kreger, then aged five, was chosen to christen the *Merrill* with a bouquet of roses instead of the traditional bottle of champagne. The drifting of rose petals downstream marked the close of a colorful and significant period in the history of the river.

Port of Portsmouth Customs Records of Outgoing Ships

Vessels built at Exeter	Tonnage	Date	Builder
Brig *Endeavour*	97	1784	
Sloop *Friendship*	39	1784	
Schooner *Jane*	75	1785	
Brig *Mary Ann*	177	1786	
Brig *Betsey*	182	1787	Eli. Giddinge
Brig *Nancy*	100	1787	Eli. Giddinge

Brig *Nancies*	165	1787	
Brig *Harriot*	135	1788	
Ship *Betsy*	191	1788	
Snow *Abigail*	152	1788	Eli. Ladd
Schooner *Antelope*	80	1788	McLure, Woodbury,
Odlin			
Ship *Arethusa*	140	1789	
Ship *Cleopatra*	301	1790	Eli. Ladd
Ship *Rainbow*	198	1790	
Brig *Arethusa*	212	1791	Sheafe
Ship *Columbia*	286	1791	Eli. Ladd
Schooner *Mars*	52	1792	John McClintock
Ship *Fame*	240	1793	Eli. Ladd
Brig *Friendship*	127	1793	Eli. Giddinge
Ship *Hercules*	498	1793	Eli. Ladd
Brig *Nancies*	129	1794	Eli. Ladd
Sloop *Squamscott*	40	1794	Jos. Gilman
Ship *Randolph*	264	1795	Hall
Brig *Neptune*	186	1795	Sheafe
Ship *Eliza*	285	1795	Eli. Ladd
Barque *Resolution*	187	1796	Nat'l. Giddinge
Ship *John*	289	1796	Benj. Boardman
Brig *Charlotte*	285	1798	Eli. Ladd
Brig *Oliver Peabody*	158	1799	Sam'l. Chamberlain
Brig *New York*	291	1799	Eli. Ladd
Brig *Planter*	142	1800	Jos. Swasey
Ship *Tom*	288	1800	Jos. Swasey
Brig *Mary*	137	1800	Thos. Savage
Ship *Hampshire*	245	1801	Jos. Swasey
Ship *Orozimbo*	264	1802	Jos. Swasey
Ship *Monticello*	211	1803	Jos. Swasey
Ship *Frances*	259	1803	Dan'l. Conner
Ship *Exeter*	291	1804	Jos. Swasey
Ship *Samaritan*	212	1804	Benj. Smith
Ship *General Eaton*	294	1805	Eli. Giddinge
Ship *Doris*	202	1805	Jos. Swasey
Schooner *Exeter Packet*	33	1806	Jos. Swasey
Ship *Roxanne*	331	1806	John Page

Ship *Maria*	287	1807	Jos. Swasey
Sloop *Nymph*	32	1816	Jos. Swasey
Sloop *Caroline*	25	1828	Jos. Fernald
Schooner *Cornelin*	71	1838	Rich'd. Currier
Sloop *Mystic*	27	1841	Wm. Willey
Sloop *Alice*	47	1872	Geo. Fernald
Schooner *Merrill*	52	1902	Stewart Russell

Some Exeter Imports

Coffee, raisins, currants, sugar, cinnamon, tea, flour, wheat, almonds, fish, oranges, salt, pepper, cloves, rum, cocoa, lemons.

Telescopes, tallow, hobby-horses, soap, glass, napkins, grindstones, brass kettles, nails, iron, clocks, hand-organs, coal, cordials, diapers, anchors, feather beds, pins, cotton, paints, indigo, duck, quills, carpets, boats, hides, hemp, warming pans, buttons, wool, lead, down pillows, quadrants, thimbles, mahogany.

Some Exeter Exports

Pine boards, barrel staves, masts, horns, oil, saddles, carriages, candles, oars, oak plankets, barrel heads and hoops, turpentine, shingles, boats, leather, shoes, hats, duck, soap, bricks.

Horses, sheep, poultry, cattle, fish, potatoes, oil, cider, beef, corn.

Some Exeter Ship's Masters

J. Trefethen, Peter Turner, Samuel Gerrish, Samuel Chauncey, Elisha Low, Samuel Chamberlain, Edward S. Young, George M. Greenough, Noah Lougee.

Listed by William G. Saltonstall, 1936.

Destinations of Exeter Ships

Rio de Janiero	Madeira
Bermuda	Dunkirk
Digby, N.S.	Oporto
St. Johns, N.B.	Guadeloupe

Liverpool	St. Croix
Cardiff	Antigua
Bristol	Cuba
London	Cayenne
Cadiz	St. Vincents
Copenhagen	Barbados
Sicily	St. Kitts
Gothenburg	Turks Island
Barcelona	St. Thomas
Stockholm	Grenada
Hamburg	Jamaica
Rotterdam	Haiti
Tenerife	

Listed by William G. Saltonstall, 1936.

CHAPTER V

❧

GOOD TIMES ON THE RIVER

The spirit of Ambrose Swasey must be smiling. Swasey's gift to the town, the Parkway, dedicated in 1931, stretching along the west bank of the Squamscott for almost a mile has never been busier.

In warm weather, from dawn to dusk, joggers, walkers, and bicyclists use its paths; senior citizens from the nearby Squamscott View Apartments rest on its benches; and parents watch as their toddlers make their uncertain way across the grass.

Once a week in summer, farmers peddle their fresh produce in the cool shade of trees set out in the pattern created by landscape architects, the Olmstead Brothers, a later generation of the designer of New York's Central Park and of Boston Gardens.

Special events are held each year on the Parkway. Since 1972, Old Home Day has been attracting hundreds to a program of children's games, parades, band concerts, and fireworks over the river. In 1983, the practice of holding Thursday evening concerts was begun, with the audience seated near the spot where once mast trees were rolled into the water to be loaded onto ships bound for Portsmouth.

It had not always been so idyllic. In previous years, boys calling themselves the "River Rats" swam, fished, and boated in water that was heavily polluted. On hot days, they dived from coal docks, and after dark, shot rats that lived in the town dump, an accumulation of trash and garbage that was gradually covering the rotting remains of the old wharves and shipyards along the river.

Swasey's gift restored to the town the scenic beauty of the Squamscott that had been lost for decades with commercial uses of the river. Federal and state laws controlling water pollution at last forced a clean-up of raw sewage. Boaters could travel down to Great Bay and beyond without

Rowing on Squamscott River. Courtesy of PEA.

being assailed by noxious odors and effluents.

Pleasure boats of one kind or another had been following the channel of the Squamscott for decades. Descriptions of downriver excursions appeared regularly in the *Exeter News-Letter* of the 1800s and the early 1900s. On July 28, 1882, for example, it was reported that "The steamer *Lottie* has been quite busy during the past week in making moonlight excursions down the river."

Once a barge had unloaded its cargo of coal, passengers could ride on the return trip to Portsmouth. They ate their lunch at Great Bay, stopped briefly in Portsmouth, then returned to Exeter by the "electrics" (trolley cars) or to Hampton by "steam cars." If they had carried along their bicycles, the more ambitious travelers sometimes cycled all the way home. When a storm blew up, passengers had to be prepared to stay overnight.

A totally new form of recreation was introduced in 1864 by a group of PEA students who bought a four-oared shell and formed a rowing club. At first, sculling was confined to the Exeter (or, as students called it, the "Upper") river. By 1881, racing by academy students on the Squamscott was considered sport. Regattas were held in June each ear, with the course extending as far as Newfields Landing.

After 1884, interest in the sport died out until its revival in 1912 when two barges and a rowing shell were acquired. Over the years, various boathouses were used, the present structure near the entrance to Swasey Parkway being dedicated in 1930. The silting in of the river is a continuing problem for the port of rowing. PEA has now abandoned inter-scholastic racing on the Squamscott because of the unpredictability of river conditions. A dredging near the boathouse by PEA in 1952 has lost its effectiveness.

Between 1899 and 1910, a group of Exeter business and professional men enjoyed the sport of motorboating on the Squamscott in 18-to 24-foot boats ranging from three to ten horsepower and fueled by gasoline. These so-called naptha launches made up what was known as the Squamscott Flotilla.

In 1905, Jacob Carlisle and Robert Kent offered a silver cup to encourage racing by owners. Dr. Wm. Nute, Wm. Seward, H.W. Anderson, Albert Willey, Forrest Wilson, Frank Peavey, R.C. Stevenson, A.S. Wetherell, James Tattersall, W.B. Folsom, and others. An *Exeter News-Letter* item on August 10, 1910 reported that a floating landing and gangway had been built at the Connors wharf for the use of the public and the more than 25 powerboat owners. By 1913 the craze had apparently died out, for there were no more references to it in the local paper.

But boating on the Squamscott was not entirely for fun. The weirs visible in coves along the river were meant for serious business. Until 1976, when weirs were declared illegal, modern fishermen used these devices, just as the Indians had, to trap shad and smelts coming upriver to spawn.

American eels were an especially profitable "crop." They were usually speared through the ice. As many as 50 to 60 pounds might be caught in a day, to be packed live into barrels and shipped to Boston and New York at holiday time. Russell Fieldsend, a veteran of more than 50 years on the river, remembers a record catch of 540 pounds of eels in one day.

Each man usually has his favorite spot for eeling. He chops a wide hole in the ice near hummocks of grass where eels hibernate in the mud. A bow-net, made of mesh and about 30 feet around, is sometimes used to trap smelt. In the coldest part of winter, fish shanties still dot the icy cover of the Squamscott. With these shelters fishermen drop their lines to hook the unwary smelt.

Clamming and oystering have been good, too, especially, in the lower Squamscott. The *Exeter News-Letter* of January 7, 1876 reported from

Fishing Through Ice. Courtesy of Exeter News-Letter.

Stratham that an oyster bed with "large-sized bivalves" had been found between the two bridges. After a day of digging out shellfish, local fishermen have often spent an evening at a riverside shack, eating their fill of steamed clams and oysters.

Each spring at Great Falls near String Bridge, alewives are collected with dip nets, just as the Indians did centuries ago. Although most people today consider alewives too bony to be edible, they have been used by farmers to fertilize hills of corn since Colonial times. Currently, alewives, gathered by the barrelful, go into lobster pots as bait.

Through the efforts of the New Hampshire Fish and Game Department, the shad, several pounds larger than the alewife, is making a comeback in Squamscott waters. Seabrown trout are also being stocked, to improve fishing for recreation. At the same time, predatory lamprey eels are being removed from the river at the rate of seven thousand per year. Fish ladders in use at the Exeter dam since 1970 and at Pickpocket since 1971 have made it easier for ocean fish to reach the pools of fresh water in which they spawn.

Netting alewives on Squamscott River. Courtesy of Exeter News-Letter.

Good Times on the River

In tribute to the alewives that came upriver in record numbers in a period of drought to save Exeter colonists from starving after crops had failed, the town fathers chose to feature the fish on the town seal.

Duck-hunting has been a popular sport on both the Exeter and the Squamscott since earliest days, when as many as 100 "great, gray geese" could be taken in a week. In the late 19th century, there was considerable commercial duck-hunting each fall. With the use of a "gunning float," an ingenious type of duck blind that looks like a piece of the riverbank, broken off and floating, hunters today have great success during the migration of wild fowl. A favorite take-off point for hunters for about 50 years has been Chapman's Landing, just below the Newfields-Stratham bridge.

All of these activities have been greatly enhanced with the construction of sewage disposal systems in towns that border the river. Exeter's system dates from 1964, and Newfields completed its sewage treatment plant in 1984. It is possible once again for swimmers to brave the currents of the Squamscott just off the Newfields shore; and an accidental fall from a motorboat or canoe is not as disagreeable as it once was. Some believe that the return of more shad and smelts signals cleaner water, but it is likely that the efforts of the Fish and Game Department have contributed a great deal to that success story.

Above the Great Falls, use of the river has always taken on a different character. Except for ice-cutting in the winter and canoe rentals in the summer, there is no history of commerce. Fishing, swimming, and skating have been traditional activities. Bass, hornpout, pickerel, and perch were once plentiful. As recently as 1955, a record-sized pickerel was caught. Henry Shute, writing in *The Real Diary of a Real Boy*, told of a happy day spent fishing with a friend all morning, then enjoying a meal of fried potatoes and fish over a campfire. "Cought 5 perch and 4 pickerel," his diary entry read.

In the years before private and public pools were at hand, the river was the only place to swim. In various reminiscences, Exeter people referred to swimming holes at the Eddy, the Gravel (near Hill Bridge), the Fisheries, the Ice House, the Elms, the Oaks, and Second Bridge.

All but the last-named and the Gravel were off-limits to girls, since the usual practice for boys was to "skinny dip." In a poem called "Down to Second," Sam Cote, an Exeter versifier of the early 20th century, vividly described the fun he had at that swimming place. He concluded with these lines:

> If I had the means
> I'd build a monument
> Out there on the ridge
> And immortalize that swimming hole
> At the old Second Bridge."

Swimming on the Exeter River was immortalized in another way by a popular work of literature by an academy alumnus, John Knowles. In *A Separate Peace*, made into a movie in 1972. Knowles built his plot around an imaginary episode that took place on a tree high above the Exeter River. One boy, by jiggling the branch, upset the other and made him jump too soon, causing an injury that later resulted in his death.

Forcing someone to take the risk of jumping into the river was not unusual. Many a boy learned to swim in this way, struggling to keep afloat by frantically dogpaddling to shore. Today, it is a custom of academy students to leap into the river at Hill Bridge while fully clothed.

A writer in the *Exeter News-Letter* of September 11, 1903 stated that he much preferred the Exeter River to the "dirty tidewater the other side of the dams." For picnicking, this writer recommended the "Eddy Woods" where picnic parties taken upriver by a 30-foot launch used to gather for ball games, boat races, and group singing before floating downstream at night. For Fourth of July celebrations at the Eddy, platforms were erected for dancing to the music of the Cornet Band after a day of feasting, tub racing, and swimming matches.

Picnics were held, too, at Gilman Park where three Civil War cannons symbolically stood watch over the confluence of the Little and Exeter Rivers. Unfortunately, one of the cannons has been destroyed by vandals. Green Gate, a popular picnic place on the river on Kensington Road, originally owned by "General" W.A. Green, was the scene of many colorful political gatherings.

Canoeing has always been an active sport, and in the past, rowboats for fishing or picnicking could be rented as well. It is not unusual to see a boatload of fishermen peacefully trolling on the river. Since 1974, the Exeter Recreation Department has sponsored canoe races between the Kingston Road Bridge and Gilman Park. As many as 50 competitors take part annually.

Fishing on the Exeter River. Matthew E. Thomas Collection.

Hunters have sought out the quiet coves of the Exeter River when duck-hunting season comes along. Nature lovers have learned to avoid the area during that period, but at other times they paddle upriver in search of unusual trees and plants, to observe beaver lodges and other aspects of animal life as well as to see the wide variety of birds. Groups of Boy Scouts have in the past set up box nests to encourage wood ducks to return to the river banks each year.

Like the Indians who preceded them by many centuries, campers come each summer to pitch their tents close to the river. The Green Gate Campground was opened in 1965; and in 1979, The Elms, located near the old swimming hole by that name, began accepting campers. Although both of these now have swimming pools, some campers still prefer a cooling dip in the river and often take canoes out to enjoy the solitude of the peaceful stream.

More adventurous canoeists attempt to follow the course of the river all the way from its source in Chester to the Great Dam, a distance of 34 miles. Portages must be made in some sections. Usually such a canoe trip is possible only when the water is high in the spring.

Libby Trail Bridge. Courtesy of PEA.

In winter, of course, the prime sport is skating. When the ice is thick and smooth, skaters go far up the river, enjoying a crisp, clear evening with a bonfire afterward to warm hands and feet. In the days when the Exeter Manufacturing Company drew off water for its operation, the edges of the river could be dangerous with thin ice ready to crack with the slightest weight.

Before indoor hockey rinks were available, practice sessions for academy students were often held near Gilman Park. Impromptu games brought fierce competition among town boys ("townies") and PEA students ("stewedcats.") Henry Shute, who as a boy had engaged in plenty of skirmishes with academy students before becoming one himself, wrote in the 1880s, "Not a boy in the neighborhood who is not dented all over with the impact of the hockey block."

Those on foot have experienced, too, the pleasures of the Exeter River. In 1916, Reverend Frederick Libby laid out the 4½-mile Libby Trail, built along the river with the aid of academy students. The trail extended from Gilman Park to a point above the eddy. At one time, a bridge of fallen logs made it possible to cross to the playing fields on the other side.

In recent years, other paths and cross-country ski trails have been developed on academy land on the east side of the river by PEA students and members of the faculty.

Although much of the Exeter River seems relatively untouched by residential development, a group known as the Exeter River Association, an outgrowth of the Rockingham Land Trust, is pressing efforts to keep the river in as natural a state as possible. One day, the Exeter River may approach a condition of cleanliness like that which prevailed before the coming of man to its banks. It will then be more desirable than ever as a place for renewal and recreation.

CHAPTER VI

❧

BACK TO THE RIVER

"The sleepy Swampscott [sic], for generations a forgotten river behind the main street, is becoming a focal point of a town quite literally turning itself around." These are the hopeful words contained in a description of the town of Exeter in the 1985-86 "Seacoast Newcomers' Guide," issued by *Portsmouth Magazine*.

It was the building of one brick block after another in the late 19th century to replace wooden shops destroyed in a series of fires, that shut the Squamscott away from the view of the passerby. Just as the river's commerce had declined, so did public awareness of this well-traveled and scenic route to the sea disappear.

No longer were goods delivered to the rear of ships along the river (although a pulley for that purpose still exists in the former Kimball's hardware store). Access to the river was not needed, as delivery wagons and later trucks brought merchandise directly to the shopkeeper at street level. From String Bridge to Swasey Parkway, only narrow passageways led to the unpaved road by the river.

Some store owners, to be sure, had installed high windows overlooking the Exeter and the Squamscott, but these often blocked from shoppers' view by shelves or counters. Only between String Bridge and High Street Bridge was the river still visible, with several wooden buildings still standing, although in need of repair.

It was not until Swasey Parkway was built that Exeter awoke to the possibility of opening the Squamscott for public use again. Ambrose Swasey's gift eliminated the unsightly town dump and rotting wharves to create a park that bordered the river and gave a pleasant access to Swasey's summer home on Newfields Road.

In spite of this fine addition to the town, Water Street, by the 1960s,

Cavil Mill, built c. 1740–1753, oldest mill still standing on the Exeter River.
Photo by Camilla Lockwood.

appeared to be dying as a commercial center. Exeter's once glorious day as a major Piscataqua port had ended long before. In the previous 50 years, the automobile and the railroad had taken their toll. Shoppers were driving to malls and shunning local stores.

A $930,000 bond issue for an anti-pollution project had been turned down by voters in 1959. With the river silted in once more, and the Newfields-Stratham bridges sealed shut, only small boats could move up and down the Squamscott. Except for Swasey Parkway, the riverfront was virtually abandoned.

In the late 1960s downtown Exeter began to come alive. The Town of Exeter Planning Board, working with consultants, presented in 1969 a general plan for the future needs of the community. These included suggestions for the rehabilitation of an area bounded by Court, Bow, and

Clifford Streets, PEA property, and the Exeter River, as well as part of Water Street and the Squamscott riverfront. The Board was concerned with "blight" along the shores of the Exeter-Squamscott River and the need to correct conditions contributing to that condition. It was the first of many studies to encourage the opening of Water Street establishments to the river.

The Chamber of Commerce, with the guidance of its executive secretary, Marcha Latwen, introduced in 1972 policies that would influence the future of that area and led to the revitalization of Water Street, String Bridge, and the waterfront. Donald S. Robie, who had formed the Exeter Investment Company in 1970, began the renovation of buildings in the upper block of Water Street, including the old firehouse. Robie's buildings, The Millworks, are located on Kimball Island, the site of Thomas Wilson's grist mill, built in 1639. The Chamber's long-term commitment was supported by both private and public sectors. Old businesses were restored and new businesses encouraged. A general cleanup of the waterfront began.

The Federal Clean Water Act, and the New Hampshire Water Pollution Act, both passed in 1972, helped to provide funds and incentives to build treatment plants. In 1973, the owner of a newly opened restaurant on Water Street placed picnic tables near the west bank of the Exeter River, the first attempt to utilize its natural beauty.

In June, 1974, the Exeter Townscape Master Plan for development of the Water Street area was presented to the town by the Exeter Area Chamber of Commerce, Town of Exeter, and the Southeastern New Hampshire Regional Planning Commission. Among other changes, it recommended a waterfront park and a new bridge to cross the Exeter River from High Street at Portsmouth Avenue to academy land near River Street. It called for improvement of the Squamscott by dredging, so that Exeter could provide "natural-oriented commercial services."

Four years later, further impetus to these developments was given when the Downtown Historic District was created by the town. This area encompassed Front Street and part of Water Street. Under terms of this agreement, exterior alterations to buildings must be reviewed by the Exeter Historic District Commission, a group which is still actively serving the town. In the same year, yet another Master Plan was presented, including uses of the waterway.

With an expanded Historic District nominated for the National

Register of Historic Places in 1980, revitalization of the waterfront began in earnest. When National Register status was granted in 1982, tax benefits made the renovation of older buildings possible. Several business blocks have now been restored and improved under terms favorable to developers.

At present, further plans are under consideration for filling in the Squamscott near the Parkway to add space for parking and for the development of walkways along the river, as well as docks for pleasure boats. Application to the U.S. Army Corps of Engineers will be made regarding the upgrading of the Squamscott by dredging. Changes in the bridge structure in Stratham to permit larger boats to come upriver are under consideration as well.

For any future use of the Squamscott, the bridges currently in place pose a serious problem. The highway bridge on Route 101 will permit the passage of fairly tall sailboats, but the present Route 108 bridge between Newfields and Stratham, and the Boston & Main railroad bridge farther downriver, allow headroom of only about three feet at mid-tide.

One of the principal obstacles to restoring the Squamscott to full recreational use was the sealing shut of bridges over the lower river. The Newfields-Stratham bridge, the so-called "Singing Bridge" (because of the sound of tires on its steel surface), was changed from a swing span to a fixed bridge in 1954 after river traffic declined to such a low level that a bridge tender was needed very seldom.

This bridge on Route 108 had been built as a wooden lift toll bridge in 1792, and was operated as such until 1907 when the county took it over. In 1926, a new steel bridge, funded by the state and county, replaced it. The span could be swung open, and until 1935 was maintained as a swing bridge with a bridge tender. In that year, the U.S. War Department ruled that nine hours' notice must be given to have the bridge opened; and soon there was almost no traffic requiring this action.

The Boston & Maine railroad bridge had ceased its operation as a lift bridge at the same time, making it impossible for any but moderate-sized boats to travel up the river. Since the railroad bridge is still used once a day by freight trains, it is unlikely that it will soon be dismantled, or that its owners would consider restoring it to the status of a lift bridge.

In one important respect, the Squamscott has been vastly improved over the days of industry and shipbuilding. As early as 1945, a survey by the State Planning Board had found the bacteria count in the Squamscott to be 170 times higher than an acceptable level. The Board recommended a sewage treatment plant and control of industrial waste disposal. A Water Pollution Board for Great Bay and its tributaries was established in 1954. When the town of Exeter finally put in a sewage treatment plant, with lagoons, into operation, town sewers no longer emptied directly into the Squamscott.

When Milliken, Inc. sold its textile plant (formerly the Exeter Manufacturing Company) in 1981 to Nike, it gave to the town its sewage treatment plant along with flowage rights to the river. At the same time, Milliken released its rights to the Great Falls dam, the King's Falls properties, Pickpocket dam, and four tracts of land along the Exeter River, of which three are in Brentwood. "For the first time in 150 years," stated an *Exeter News-Letter* article, "the town took control of the river."

In 1985, work was begun in Exeter on a joint federal-state $1,000,000 project for sewage and drainage to improve existing systems by separating storm drains from town sewer lines. In the same year, Newfields opened its second-stage sewage treatment plant. Now it remains only for Stratham to develop a program to remove from the entire Squamscott evidences of man's misuse of the river.

Someone has said that the quality of life of a community depends on the quality of its water. The quality of a river depends on the dedication of the residents along its banks to the preservation and restoration of its natural beauty.

No one can say where a river really begins nor exactly where it ends. "The origin and the mouth of the river are present everywhere along its banks," wrote Unitarian minister Donald Marshall in a 1983 sermon. "It rolls endlessly onward, droplet and stream, this week's rain mixed with last year's artesian along its course, yet the river remains itself. It changes constantly, yet always becomes itself."

The Exeter-Squamscott will be here long after the last resident has departed, just as it was here long before man came. Whether it can return to its pristine state is a question we must all address. Perhaps an understanding of its gift to us over the centuries and the debt we owe it will encourage us to preserve this priceless heritage for the generations to come.

AFTERWORD

A river does not just happen; it has a beginning and an end. Its story
is written in rich earth, in ice, and in water-carved stone, and its story
as the lifeblood of the land is filled with color, music and thunder.
                                   —Andy Russell, *The Life of a River*

As this quote from Canadian writer Andy Russell suggests, the
Exeter/Squamscott River is a dramatic storyteller, but it can also be future
teller of sorts. By examining the water and lands of the entire watershed,
from its headwaters in Chester to the end of the Great Bay Estuary in
Portsmouth, careful observers can identify trends in watershed health and
paint a picture of the river that informs future stewardship.

In 2003 the New Hampshire Estuaries Project published the *State of*
the Estuaries report that examined key environmental indicators of the
state's coastal watersheds. Many indicators suggested a system in recov-
ery. In the Squamscott River and in Great Bay during the last ten years,
the report noted that fecal coliform bacteria levels have decreased, which
suggests that improvements to wastewater treatment facilities are helping.
Harmful toxic contaminants such as PCBs, DDT, and mercury are
diminishing too, thanks to strict state and federal regulations.

But not all of the report's news was good. Oyster beds in Great Bay
have experienced a dramatic decline due primarily to oyster diseases.
Nitrogen concentrations in Great Bay are on the rise, however, the
Squamscott River has been relatively stable. And perhaps the most alarm-
ing trend is the increase in "sprawl-type" development that is occurring in
the Seacoast area. Studies from other regions suggest that if the 10% of
land is covered with hard built surfaces, such as pavement, cement or roof
tops, the water bodies around that land will have lower water quality,
resulting largely from polluted stormwater runoff. Two of the towns
touched by the Squamscott/Exeter River watershed are already more than
10% covered with hard built surfaces. Three more communities are in
imminent danger of exceeding the 10% threshold. Watershed communities must consider development designs that build cluster structures away
from critical water resources if the river is to be spared environmental
stress.

The Exeter/Squamscott River has been a river of many uses and abuses. It is thanks to concerned citizens, environmental organizations, state and federal governments, and the federal Clean Water Act of 1972, that the river and the associated Great Bay Estuary is in the best environmental condition it has been in 250 years. The river's water quality has improved, however, careful planning is still needed to ensure that this valuable natural resource will have a healthy future.

Dave Kellam
New Hampshire Estuary Project

From the source to the sea. Photo by Michael H. Heaton.

BIBLIOGRAPHY

Adams, John P. *The Piscataqua River Gundalow*. Durham, N.H.; 1982.

_____, *Drowned Valley*. Hanover, N.H.; University Press of New England, 1976.

*AMC River Guide: New Hampshire, Vermon*t. Boston: Appalachian Mountain Club, 1983.

Bachman, Ben. *Upstream, a Voyage on the Connecticut River*. Boston: Houghton Mifflin, 1985.

Bailey, Lillian. *Up and Down New Hampshire*. Orford, N.H.: Equity Publishing, 1960.

Bell, Charles, *Exeter in 1776*. Exeter, N.H.: News-Letter Press, 1876.
History of Exeter. Boston: Farwell, 1888.
Men and Things of Exeter. Exeter, N.H.: News-Letter Press, 1871 (?)

Brentwood Historical Society. *Brentwood's 225 Years, 1742-1967*. Brentwood, N.H.: 1935. New Ed. 1967.

Brewster, C.W. *Brewster's Rambles About Portsmouth*. Portsmouth, N.H.; L.W. Brewster, 1869

Chapelle, Howard S. *History of American Sailing Ships*. N.Y.; Norton, 1935.

Chapman, Donald. "New Hampshire's Landscape: How It Was Formed." *N.H. Profiles*, Jan. 1974.

Clark, Charles E. *The Eastern Frontier*, N.Y.: Knopf, 1970

Cronon, William. *Changes in the Land*. N.Y.: Hill & Wang, 1983.

Crosbie, Laurence. *The Phillips Exeter Academy: a History*. Exeter, N.H.; Plimpton Press, 1923.

Dudley, Albertus T. *In Wheelright's Day*. (Pamphlet) Exeter, N.H.; Exeter Historical Society, 1931.

Earle, Alice. *Home Life in Colonial Days*. N.Y.: Grosset & Dunlap, 1898.

Easton, Howard & Saltonstall, William, eds. *Accounts of Exeter*. 1750-1800. (Pamphlet) Exeter, N.H.: News-Letter Press, 1938.

Exeter Area Chamber of Commerce. *The Exeter Story*. (Pamphlet) 1982.

Exeter News-Letter Various issues, 1888-1985. Card-indexed at Exeter Historical Society.

Fitts, James. *History of Newfields*. Concord, N.H.: Rumford Press, 1912.

Ford, Daniel. "Story of Exeter Towne." *N.H. Profiles*, Jan. 1960.

Forrest, Edwin. "The Exeter of Today." *Granite Monthly*, Oct., 1899.

Gallup, Ronald. *Algonquian New Hampshire*. Concord, N.H.: Quarryside, 1970.

Garvin, James & Merrill, Nancy. "Exeter: Its Architectural Heritage." *N.H. Profiles*, June 1971.

George, Nellie P. *Old Newmarket*. Exeter, N.H.: News-Letter Press, 1932.

Getchell, Sylvia F. *Lamprey River Village, the Early Years*. Newmarket, N.H.:Newmarket Press 1976.

Gilman, Robbins. *The Old Logg House by the Bridge*. Portsmouth, N.H.: Peter E. Randal Publisher, 1985.

Jorgensen, Neil. *A Guide to New England's Landscape*. Chester, Conn.: Pequot Press, 1977.

Knowles, John. *A Separate Peace*. N.Y.: Bantam, 1960.

Ladd, Richard J. *New Hampshire Past and Present*. Seabrook, N.H.: Withey Press, 1977.

Lamson, Everett. *One Backward Glance*. Barre, Vt.: 1980.

Lane, Samuel. "A Journal for the Years 1739-1803." (Pamphlet) Stratham, N.H.

Merrill, Nancy. "The Falls of the Exeter River." *Exeter News-Letter*, July 22, 1981.

New Hampshire Archaeologist. Concord, N.H.: Nos. 14, 15, 18, 23, 25.

Pennacook Inter-Tribal Nation. "Historic Indian-Colonial Relations." (Pamphlet) Concord, N.H.: 1977.

Perry, William G. *Exeter in 1830*. Exeter, N.H.: News-Letter Press, 1913.

Phillips, John "Exeter, N.H." *New England Magazine*, Vol 41, 1910.

Phillips Exeter Academy. *Bulletin*, Mar., 1912; Oct., 1917; Aug., 1927.

Russell, Howard S. *Indian New England Before the Mayflower.* Hanover, N.H.: University Press of New England, 1980.

Saltonstall, William G. *Ports of Piscataqua.* N.Y.: Russell, 1941.

_____, "Shipbuilding at Exeter." PEA *Bulletin,* Oct., 1936.

_____, " Shipping and Shipbuilding on the Exeter River." Paper delivered at Exeter Historical Society, Jan. 14, 1936.

Shute, Henry. *Neighborhood Sketches.* Exeter, N.H.: News-Letter Press, 1901.

_____, *A Real Diary of a Real Boy.* Dublin, N.H.: Bauhan, 1967.

_____, *Sequil.* Boston: Everett Press, 1904.

Silver, Helenette. *N.H. Game & Furbearers, a History.* (Pamphlet) Concord, N.H.: N.H. Fish & Game Dept., 1957.

Society for the Preservation of New England Antiquities. *Old Time New England,* Nos. 2, 60.

Stilgoe, John. *Common Landscape of America,* 1580-1845. New Haven, Conn.: Yale University Press, 1982.

Thomas, Matthew. *Original Territory of Historic Exeter,* Portsmouth: Randall Press, 1976.

Thompson, Mary P. *Landmarks in Ancient Dover.* Durham, N.H.: Durham Historical Society, 1965.

Trigger, Bruce, ed. *Handbook of North American Indians,* Vol. 15. Washington, D.C.: Smithsonian Institution, 1978-

Wallis, Wilson & Ruth. *The MicMac Indians of Eastern Canada.* Minneapolis: University of Minnesota Press, 1954.

Webber, Laurence. "Shipbuilding on the Piscataqua." *N.H. Profiles,* June 1971.

Winslow, Richard E. *The Piscataqua Gundalow.* Portsmouth Marine Society, 1983.

Wood, Pamela. "The Almost Forgotten Boathouse." *Rowing USA.* April/May, 1983.

INDEX

❧

ABOUT THE AUTHOR

Olive (Richards) Tardiff, born in Exeter in 1916, has been writing about Exeter and New Hampshire history since 1972. She grew up within walking distance of the Exeter-Squamscott River, and in the 1980s began to explore its history.

The Exeter-Squamscott: River of Many Uses is the result of the extensive research through which Ms. Tardiff gained both respect and affection for the river which has served so many generations so well. Olive Tardiff has published five paperback books dealing with Exeter and New Hampshire history, served as editor of *On Ever, Robinson*, the history of Robinson Female Seminary, and contributed to Nancy Merrill's *History of Exeter, 1888-1988*.

The Exeter River Watershed

The Exeter River rises from a group of spring-fed ponds in Chester, New Hampshire, and flows thirty-three miles to downtown Exeter where it changes its name to the Squamscott River and becomes a tidal, primary tributary to Great Bay. The river often meanders, frequently doubling back on itself, and passes through several short stretches of rapids in Brentwood before falling over the dam in Exeter.

The Exeter River watershed covers approximately 67,700 acres of Rockingham County. The watershed includes sizeable portions of ten municipalities including Chester, Sandown, Danville, Fremont, Raymond, Brentwood, East Kingston, Kingston, Kensington, and Exeter.

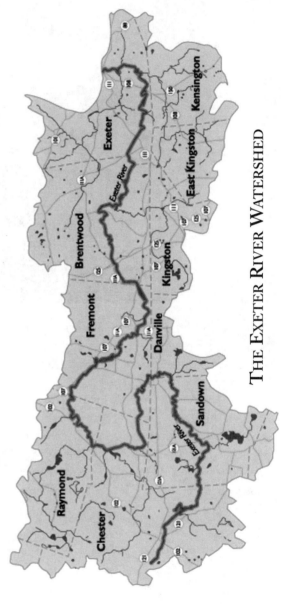

THE EXETER RIVER WATERSHED